Survival Fundraising

for small not-for-profits

A new action guide
for raising money in tough times

Donald L. Ruhl

Library of Congress Cataloging-in-Publication Data
Ruhl, Donald L., 1935
Survival Fundraising for small not-for-profits:
A new action guide for raising money in touch times

ISBN: 978-0-692-00894-2

Library of Congress Control Number: 2010927629

First Published in 2010

Turnstone Press, LLC
Rye, NH

Cover design by Raleigh Design

Printed in the United States of America

This book is dedicated to Ellen Ruhl without whose support the book would not have been written

and

Dr. Howard Brown, co-author of *Breakthrough Management for Not-for-Profit Organizations: Beyond Survival in the 21st Century*, for his many contributions to this project.

Acknowledgments

A book is the result of the input of many people who have contributed in a variety of ways. Of special significance were the contributions of my wife, Ellen Ruhl, and Dr. Howard Brown.

Professionals who have been heavily involved in the fundraising process who have contributed to the book are: Thomas Bentley, Joseph Bevilacqua, Susan Bunting, Lewis Feldstein, Robert Hatem, William Klenk, Byron Matthews, Jay McGovern, Jonathan Miller, Frank Novak, Jean Poth, Ann Powell, Timothy Schiavoni, and David Thomas.

The author wishes to thank the following individuals who have served as his mentors over an extended period of time: Jack Armstrong, Ken Benne, Harold Bentley, Joseph Bevilacqua, Paul Bevilacqua, Charles Billups, William Cavallaro, John Dimitry, Eugene DuBois, Ferd Ensinger, Joseph Giampa, Malcolm Knowles, Arthur Levine, Stuart Marshall, Barry Oshry, Gene Phillips, Robert Ramsey, John Ravekes, Lowell Trowbridge, Ed Veasey, and Robert Webber.

Family and friends who have been particularly supportive of the author who are deserving of special recognition are: Ellen Ruhl, Beth and Dean Wills, Heather and Walter Kinsey, Richard and Margee Ruhl, Michael Ruhl, Steven Ruhl, Helen and Luther Ruhl, Jacob Ruhl, Richard Winslow III, Richard and Virginia Winslow, John and Sylvia Mattis, Russell, Violet, Tony, and Ann Longenecker, Howard and Nancy Brown, Gene and Rita Grillo, Jim Swarr, Joyce King, Nick and Barbara Hornyak, Herb and Marge Phillips, William and Dee Nofsker, Ed and Zoe Veasey, Roderick Condon II, and John and Mary Katsaros.

Participants in the printing and publishing process have been: Ellen Ruhl, Howard Brown, Eric Valentine, John and Sarah Raleigh of Raleigh Design, Kumar Persad of Tri-State Associated Services, John Katsaros, Dean Wills, and Reggy Roycroft.

About the Author

Dr. Donald Ruhl is an organizational consultant specializing in not-for-profit organizations. He is Dean Emeritus of the College at Northern Essex Community College (Mass.) and the former President of Garrett Community College in Maryland. Dr. Ruhl served for fifteen years as the Executive Director and then President of the Greater Haverhill Chamber of Commerce in Massachusetts. His 19 years of experience as the CEO of not-for-profit organizations along with his chairmanship and membership on a variety of not-for-profit Boards has given him the "on the firing line" expertise to write *Survival Fundraising.*

Dr. Ruhl is the co-author of the pioneering book, *Breakthrough Management For Not-For-Profit Organizations: Beyond Survival in the 21st Century* (Brown and Ruhl-Praeger-2003). Dr. Arthur Levine, former President of Teachers College, Columbia University, said of the book, "Brown and Ruhl have managed to produce an extraordinary volume that could become a new standard text both for individuals considering the not-for-profit field and those who are already professionals in the field."

Dr. Ruhl and his wife, Ellen, reside in New Hampshire and Florida.

Table of Contents

Introduction

Reasons for Writing this Book

Survival Fundraising shows a small not-for-profit organization how to break through fundraising inertia to create a unique organization with an important, compelling mission that successfully raises money in tough times.

Survival Fundraising as the title states, deals with survival. It is not the typical fundraising book that leaves the reader with impractical solutions to unimportant issues. It deals with the essentials of financial survival through fundraising.

Survival Fundraising is a book written specifically for the large number of small not-for-profit organizations that exist in every city and town in the United States and increasingly around the world. These organizations have unique fundraising problems which are specifically addressed by *Survival Fundraising*.

Survival Fundraising is new. It is not the same old boring business-as-usual fundraising book that fails to deliver on its promises. *Survival Fundraising* is new in concept and design. It is written for the new world of not-for-profit fundraising.

Survival Fundraising is an action guide. Its purpose is to show the reader how to take action to raise badly needed money. The aim of this book is to promote immediate action that gets fundraising results.

Survival Fundraising is geared to raising money in tough times. Because it deals with overcoming THE SIX MAJOR BARRIERS TO SUCCESSFUL FUNDRAISING, it provides answers to your fundraising problems in the worst of economic times. Unique not-for-profit organizations with compelling missions are organizations that successfully raise money in tough times. This book shows you how to be such an organization.

Small not-for-profit organizations generally exhibit certain characteristics regarding their fundraising efforts. They are less able to afford a full-time fundraising professional or consultants, have less historical fundraising experience, and lack the organizational back-up and other resources to mount and sustain a fundraising effort. They also tend to be emergency focused rather than strategically focused and to suffer from fundraising inertia because of a small overworked staff. In addition, many small not-for-profit organizations are less able to do the necessary fundraising research and are less visible in the communities they serve.

How to Use this Book

The author, in the process of working on *Breakthrough Management for Not-for-Profit Organizations: Beyond Survival in the 21ˢᵗ Century* with Howard Brown (Praeger, 2003), came to realize that there are SIX MAJOR BARRIERS to successful fundraising. THE SIX MAJOR BARRIERS are: (1) being like everyone else, (2) having a non-participating Board, (3) reacting only to emergencies, (4) going it alone, (5) communicating the wrong message, and (6) participating in one-shot efforts. Each of the six chapters in *Survival Fundraising* shows you how to overcome one of these SIX MAJOR BARRIERS.

Each chapter in *Survival Fundraising* is intended to be short enough to be read in one sitting. This allows the reader to concentrate on a specific aspect of the fundraising process, relate it to one's own experience, and then take a break before moving on. This break provides important time to think about how the ideas presented can be implemented in one's own organization.

Every effort has been made to involve the reader in an active way in the content of each chapter. Each chapter begins with a series of important questions for the reader to consider. A ❏ *to talk about. . .,* ❏ *to think about. . .,* ❏ *to carry out. . .* format provides an exciting framework for reader participation. Each chapter serves as a guide for thought and action and is designed to enhance one's decision making in the areas being discussed. Practical solutions are provided to generate more income in tough economic times. All of the chapters discuss important ways in which one can create a sustainable fundraising process.

Finally...

It is the hope of the author that *Survival Fundraising* will provide a new and exciting framework for your fundraising efforts as a small not-for-profit organization. It is his hope that you will quickly develop a strategic plan that will get you started right now to create a unique organization with an important, compelling mission that successfully raises the money you need; an organization that is not the same old boring business-as-usual kind of organization that drives off donors. Use *Survival Fundraising* to create a process that will serve as your GPS for fundraising, moving quickly and decisively, utilizing the advantages you have as a small not-for-profit to exceed your fundraising goals.

Use *Survival Fundraising* to help you to prove that your organization and the work that it does is a necessity that must be supported. Use the book as a guide to help to create a Board that has the will and the strategic skills to build a unique organization that will attract committed enthusiastic donors. Use the book as well to identify, involve, and work with groups of potential donors.

Good luck in starting immediately to build a culture that sustains the fundraising efforts of your small not-for-profit organization over time.

Chapter 1

Creating a Differentiated Organization— The Key to Raising Money

Important Questions

❏ *1-1: to think about . . .*

➤ How do you avoid being the same old boring business-as-usual type of organization that no one wants to support financially?

➤ How do you create an organization that is unique, important and exciting, that motivates people to provide you with money and other resources?

➤ How can you be certain that your organization is really conspicuously different in an important, positive way from your fundraising competitors?

➤ How do you identify and learn about potential donors who believe in your unique and important philosophy, vision, and mission?

What Do We Mean by Differentiation, and Why Is It Important in Attracting Donors?

❏ *1-2: to talk about . . .* Differentiation is at the heart of the fundraising and resource development process. But what do we mean by differentiation and why is it important?

When we talk about differentiation we are talking about being conspicuously different from one's competitors in a positive sense. Later in this chapter we will discuss specific ways in which you can create a unique motivating identity for your organization. This is of the greatest importance since many smaller not-for-profit organizations lack a distinctive and compelling vision and mission. These organizations believe that they are unique but the reality is that they are basically like everyone else.

In the present landscape of not-for-profit organizations, a rapidly growing number of not-for-profits are competing for existing resources. This increased competition makes positive organizational differentiation a prerequisite for successful fundraising. ***One does not want to be like everyone else. Duplication of effort does not inspire giving.*** It is critically important to be conspicuously different in a positive sense if one is to attract and keep excited and committed donors. Differentiation is the only way to go in today's highly competitive fundraising environment.

Build an Organizational Culture that Creates and Supports Differentiation

❏ *1-3: to carry out . . .*

1. Develop Committed Leadership

How does an organization go about differentiating itself from other organizations that are competing for the same scarce resources? The *leadership of the organization* is of critical importance in this effort. We are talking here about leadership that is dispersed throughout the organization. The Board and CEO are the principal driving forces of this leadership dispersion process.

The leadership process should take place within the following action framework.

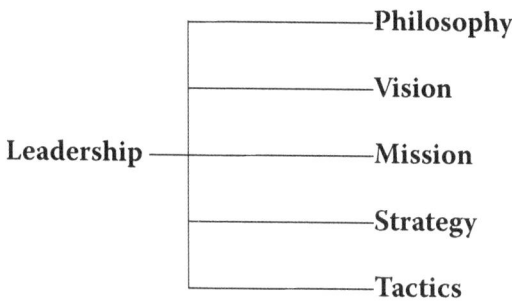

```
                        ┌───────────Philosophy
                        │
                        ├───────────Vision
                        │
Leadership ─────────────┼───────────Mission
                        │
                        ├───────────Strategy
                        │
                        └───────────Tactics
```

2. What Do You Believe In?

The philosophy of the Board, particularly its Chair and that of the CEO, concerning questions such as the following, forms the basis for the organization's efforts to differentiate itself.

- ➢ Are people inherently worthy?
- ➢ What makes life worth living?
- ➢ Is it important to help people realize their potential?
- ➢ How important is it to help people have better health?
- ➢ Are people capable of changing their behavior?
- ➢ How important is it to get resources to the people who need them most?
- ➢ Are individuals capable of self-directed learning?
- ➢ What are the inherent rights of each individual?
- ➢ What is meant by equal justice under the law?

Please note that all of these questions relate to improving the human condition which is the work of not-for-profit organizations. The leadership's philosophy concerning important questions such as these will determine the ways in which the organization's vision is conceptualized, shaped, articulated, implemented, and differentiated. Philosophy drives vision. The importance of the philosophy of an organization concerning important societal and organizational issues is frequently overlooked or underemphasized. It is important that a not-for-profit organization clearly identifies and communicates the underlying philosophy upon which the vision is based. The institutional philosophy needs to be understood and embraced throughout the organization. From this philosophy a congruent vision can then be created.

How does one develop an organizational philosophy that resonates with all the members of the organization? A philosophy that excites and motivates people to develop a differentiated vision that has emotional and intellectual impact. A philosophy and vision which a variety of stakeholders will identify with and endorse through their financial contributions.

Broad based, focused participation is required in implementing a philosophy that makes your organization a distinctive differentiated organization. Participation engenders commitment. When the audience participates, the applause is always louder. Employees who find they can't enthusiastically endorse the underlying philosophy of the organization should seek employment elsewhere. When recruiting new employees the philosophy of the organization should be clearly described. Potential employees whose philosophical beliefs do not fit the stated philosophy of the organization should not be hired. Differentiation requires a willingness to repel in order to attract. One needs to have an organization of believers if one is to achieve outstanding results. What is needed are believers who are open to an ongoing examination of the internal and external environments in which they work. Believers whose thinking on important issues is open to examination.

It is important that you examine your philosophy about life's important issues as they impact the human condition. Is your philosophy concerning these issues congruent with the philosophy of the not-for-profit organization for which you work? Does your organization clearly communicate its philosophy? Do the various stakeholders of the organization know about and understand this philosophy? Do they embrace it? Does it drive their contributions to the organization?

3. Envision Your Future Direction

With the organization's philosophy clearly in mind regarding important human development and societal issues, the next step is to be certain that the organization's vision is clear, motivating and differentiated. Vision deals with future direction. It represents an ideal future that has some realistic possibility of achievement. Vision should include a timeframe for action.

4. Know What Business You Are In

Before a not-for-profit organization can create a vision for the future, it is essential that it know what specific kind of human improvement work it wants to be in. Ted Levitt, in his classic article, entitled "Marketing Myopia," makes the point that most people in business don't know what business they are in, and if they do, they tend to define it too narrowly. Levitt illustrates this point with the example of the railroads who thought they were in the railroad business rather than the transportation business; and the telephone company which thought it was in the telephone business rather than the communications business. The issue of what business a not-for-profit organization perceives itself as being in is of critical importance because it determines what the organization does and how it behaves.

An example of this would be a college which perceives itself being in the student learning business rather than the teaching business. An emphasis on the student rather than on the teacher could make a world of difference in how the educational experience is approached. Being in the student learning business opens up an expanded number of possibilities.

Other examples of how differing perceptions of the business you're in can effect what an organization does are: a shelter for the homeless that perceives itself as being in the economic development business rather than the poverty business; a nursing home that sees itself being in the life enhancement business as opposed to the caretaker business; a history museum that perceives itself in the entertainment business rather than the historical preservation business, or a health club that perceives itself as being in the personal development business rather than the muscle building business.

5. Have an Appropriate Mission Statement Developed

With its philosophy clearly in mind, an understanding of the business it is in, and its vision articulated, a not-for-profit organization is ready to develop its mission statement. Mission deals with purpose. Mission deals with the ongoing reason the organization exists. Mission indicates how the organization is going to achieve its vision. It explains what business the not-for-profit organization is in and how it is going to serve its customers. It is important to remember that organizational philosophy, the business one is in, vision, and mission should be congruent; they should be pointing the organization in the same direction. It is this clear, differentiated sense of direction in improving the human condition that makes a not-for-profit organization attractive to its present and potential donors.

Become First in the Minds of Donors— Through Differentiation!

❑ *1-4: to think about . . .*

> ➢ How do you specifically achieve differentiation in the direction your organization is taking from the direction other organizations are taking?

> ➢ How does your organization become first in the minds of donors and potential donors in the particular category of human improvement activity in which you have chosen to excel?

It is important to begin this discussion with the point just mentioned that we are attempting to become first in the minds of donors and potential donors in the particular category of human improvement activity in which we have chosen to excel. We are using the word "donor" here in the comprehensive sense of any organization or individual who contributes financial or non-financial resources. Another term that needs to be defined as part of our discussion of specific differentiators is the term "product." In marketing the term product includes goods which are largely tangible and services which are largely intangible. As mentioned previously, not-for-profit organizations deal primarily with providing services to improve the human condition.

Following are a number of differentiators which you can use to create a unique motivating image for your organization in the minds of present and potential donors.

1. Beliefs and Values

Your not-for-profit organization needs to clearly communicate its beliefs and values if it is to attract donors who share these beliefs and values. Remember that not-for-profit organizations which make it possible for donors to achieve goals and objectives that they can't achieve on their own become highly attractive to these donors. It is essential that a not-for-profit organization know what it values and what it believes and that it act accordingly. Having convictions and holding firm to them takes courage. It means that some potential donors will be repelled. It also means, however, that significant donors who embrace your cause are more likely to step up and support your organization in major ways. Being wishy-washy about what your organization stands for is not a good way to instill confidence in potential donors.

2. Organizational Mission

Your organizational mission is a major differentiator for donors. Donors want to know how your not-for-profit organization is going to improve the human condition. Mission deals with purpose and the purpose of your organization needs to be perceived by donors as important, exciting, and unique. It is this perception of the importance of your mission that will drive donor contributions to your organization. Building a strong connection between the mission of the not-for-profit organization and the interests of the donor is essential to successful fundraising. Communication about your organizational mission must have clarity and impact. It must motivate and excite the donor! Vague generalities will not do the job.

3. People

The people in your not-for-profit organization can constitute a major differentiator in attracting donor support. The major question is: What do you want your employees to be known for as they support the mission of your not-for-profit organization? Do you want them to be known for their specialized expertise, their friendliness to customers, their superb teamwork, their commitment to mission, or to demonstrate excellence in some other facet of organizational life and performance. It is, of course, the people who will determine what kind of organization you will have and ultimately its attractiveness to potential donors. As you create a differentiated organization that will support your mission to the greatest extent possible, thereby attracting enthusiastic donors, you will want to add people who will give you the desired organizational focus.

4. Quality

There are those who argue that we will arrive at a time when the level of quality will no longer be a differentiator between organizations. The argument goes that one will have to achieve the highest quality in order to survive in the marketplace and therefore everyone will operate with high quality. Although this may be true at some distant time in the future, it certainly is not true today. Some not-for-profit organizations perform with little quality, others with average quality, and still others at a level of very high quality. High quality performance is a strong motivator for donors to contribute to your organization. If you had to choose between giving financial support to an organization of poor quality or one of high quality, in the human improvement work in which you are interested, which would you support?

High quality performance can be demonstrated in a variety of ways. Product quality, customer service quality, teamwork quality, leadership quality, community relations quality and other examples of quality make a major impact on donor perceptions of the organization. Quality consistency is of paramount importance. Quality should be built into the culture of your organization so that it can be sustained over an extended period of time. Donors are impressed and excited when they know that the organization they are supporting financially has a continuing history of serving its clients at the highest level of quality.

5. Style

The way you do things can be an important differentiator in influencing potential donors to contribute to your organization rather than to someone else. It is important to have a unified style in which different facets of your organizational behavior fit together to give you a distinctive way of doing things. In order to attract donors your style has to be highly visible and it has to be consistent. It cannot be the same old business-as-usual style that so many organizations exhibit. Your style may be characterized by your ability to provide the unexpected, to go beyond the minimal expectations of the customer. Perhaps it is the appearance of employee uniforms, office furnishings, and company vehicles that gives you a unique style. It may be the enthusiasm, commitment, and dedication of your employees that gives your organization its distinctive style. Whatever it is, your organizational style is important in attracting or repelling certain donors and in differentiating you from other organizations with which you are competing for financial and non-financial resources. You should endeavor to create an organizational style that is consistent with your mission and that enhances its attractiveness to potential donors.

6. Technology

The ways in which you utilize technology in pursuit of your mission can have a significant impact on the perceptions of potential donors. The goal, of course, is to be first in the minds of donors as a worthy recipient of their financial support. Donors will be favorably impressed if they perceive that you are operating effectively using the latest appropriate technology. The utilization of technology in developing and delivering products and services, in communicating what you are doing, in providing networks of supporting resources, in creating state of the art facilities, and in other aspects of your operation can be a major differentiating factor in attracting donors.

Using technology effectively gives your organization the image of being up to date and of knowing what it is doing. Since many organizations use technology badly, your organization will stand out from its competitors in the quest to secure donor support. Communications technology can be an important factor in providing feedback from current and potential donors about ways in which the products and services offered by your not-for-profit organization can be even more helpful to your clients. Such donor involvement will in many cases strengthen their resolve to contribute to your organization.

7. Delivery Systems

The manner in which goods and services are delivered is another important way in which your small not-for-profit organization can differentiate itself in the eyes of current and potential donors. An understanding of the marketing term, utility, is important in this regard. Utility means the want-satisfying power of a good or service. Time and place utility are of special relevance when we talk about the delivery systems of not-for-profit organizations as differentiating factors in donor perceptions. Time utility refers to providing goods and services in a timely manner. Place utility refers to providing these goods and services at places where they can be readily accessed. If the not-for-profit's delivery systems don't meet the needs of their clients in a timely manner where they can be accessed, the organizational mission will not be successful and donor perceptions will be negative. As mentioned elsewhere in this book, the Salvation Army has a long standing image of providing goods and services to those in need, in a timely manner, and at accessible places. The result is that the Salvation Army is one of the most respected not-for-profit organizations in the United States. Its image of providing goods and services in a timely effective manner results in financial support from large numbers of committed, enthusiastic donors. The manner in which goods and services are provided is one of the most visible components of the operation of a not-for-profit organization. For this reason, perceptions of not-for-profit delivery systems can be a major factor influencing donor behavior.

Differentiators

1. How Many Differentiators Should You Use?

❏ *1-5: to think about* . . . A central issue in creating a unique identity is *the number of differentiators a not-for-profit organization plans to use.* The idea behind the Unique Selling Proposition (USP) developed by Rosser Reeves is that there should be one powerful differentiator that your organization is known for that enables it to be first in the minds of the donors in your category of human improvement activity. The advantage of having one powerful differentiator that is communicated consistently over an extended period of time is that it increases the probability that your organization will achieve this number one position in the minds of donors.

If you choose to create more than one differentiator for your organization, the supplemental differentiators should support and reinforce the principal differentiator. If this is not the case your organizational image can easily become blurred and confused. With your differentiated image destroyed you will no longer be first in the minds of your donors. The advantage of having supplemental differentiators that support your major differentiator is that a greater range of donors from more segments of the donor market may be reached. One of the most powerful motivators in giving is to be able to achieve results that one could not achieve on one's own. If potential donors perceive your organization as being able to improve the human condition in areas in which they are personally interested, thus expanding the impact of their dollars, they will most likely contribute. Supplemental differentiators allow a greater number of potential donors to relate to the work of your organization. Identification with a supplemental differentiator then leads donors to identify with the central powerful differentiator.

2. Use of Supplemental Differentiators

❏ *1-6: to carry out . . .* As you create an important, motivating, differentiated identity for your organization, you may wish to further strengthen this identity by creating some supplemental differentiators that support and reinforce it.

Your Organization

1. On What Basis is Your Organization Differentiated?

❏ *1-7: to carry out . . .* Earlier in this chapter possible differentiators were identified that you can use to make your organization unique and distinctive. Building on these examples, the following action statements provide a structure for analyzing in some detail the specific basis on which your organization is differentiated. This is important as many organizations believe that they are unique and distinctive when this is not in fact the case. Reviewing these statements will enable you to fine tune the degree of emphasis that you wish to give to each of them. You may also decide that some of these action strategies are not appropriate for your organization to pursue in its quest to become a unique, important, and exciting organization that serves as a magnet for potential donors.

____ The most important benefit, or bundle of benefits, that we offer is unique and important.

____ We have a specialized niche and are dominant in it.

____ Our use of technology strengthens our ability to be unique and distinctive.

____ The people in our organization are a key ingredient in our being a unique and superior service provider.

____ We possess outstanding product knowledge, and are able to communicate this product knowledge to stakeholders and potential donors.

____ The processes by which we create our products are different from and better than the processes used by other service providers in our field. These process differences can be communicated in order to be understood.

____ We have developed a reputation as an innovator and pioneer; as an organization that is always on the cutting edge.

____ We manage the marketing process in a distinctive, compelling, effective manner. Our message is powerful, important, clear, and consistent. Our service delivery systems enhance our unique and important mission.

____ A distinctive set of beliefs and values drive our mission. They are important and motivating, and we impart them continually through spoken and unspoken means.

_____ We are willing to repel potential donors in order to attract those who identify strongly with our beliefs and values.

_____ Our distinguished track record over an extended period of time has been communicated effectively to potential donors.

_____ We operate in distinctive ways that translate into superior service for our constituents. Our distinctive manner of operating is a positive force in attracting donors.

_____ Distinguished, differentiated organizations that do important human improvement work in our field of service work with us on a regular basis, thereby increasing our impact and propelling us into a service leadership position.

_____ We use our interaction with the community to achieve a differentiated, competitive advantage in attracting donors to support our mission.

2. Are You Really Differentiated?

❏ *1-8: to carry out . . .* After you have implemented your organizational differentiators, it is time to apply the following "Seven Tests of Differentiation" in order to determine whether your organization is truly differentiated. Remember that being conspicuously different in a positive sense is essential to successful fundraising. This is especially true for smaller not-for-profit organizations that lack the capacity to provide high volume services benefitting from economy of scale. Smaller not-for-profit organizations that fail to develop unique, important, and exciting missions are almost always in a state of fiscal turmoil. Use the "Seven Tests of Differentiation" on a continuing basis in order to be certain that your organization is doing unique and important work.

3. The Seven Tests of Differentiation

❏ *1-9: to talk about . . .*

1. The one powerful, central differentiator has been consistently communicated in a clear, simple, motivating way that involves both the intellect and the emotions.

2. There are supplemental differentiators that support and strengthen the one central powerful differentiator.

3. We have received consistent, ongoing feedback that the organization and its services are conspicuously different in a positive sense.

4. We are receiving contributions of financial and non-financial resources in greater volume.

5. Our donor list is increasing and we feel they are giving because of our important, powerful, and motivating positive, differentiated image and its impact on the human condition.

6. Our donors are telling us that they strongly identify with the beliefs and values that form the core of our differentiation.

7. People are telling us that they don't believe in the beliefs and values that form the core of our differentiation.

Donors

1. Consider the Differentiated Donor

❏ *1-10: to think about . . .* Chapter 3 deals with establishing the fundraising and resource development priorities for your not-for-profit organization. Prior to doing that it will be necessary for you to identify and learn about the potential donors who are especially receptive to the differentiated philosophy, vision, and mission of your organization. You are looking for potential donors who perceive your organization as being able to assist them in achieving important goals and objectives that they can't achieve on their own. Donors who believe in you and feel passionately about the distinctive and important work that you do. Donors who support you because you are not the same old ho-hum, business-as-usual not-for-profit organization but an organization that is doing its work in an important, distinctive, and creative way. How do you find these potential donors who strongly identify with the uniqueness of your organizational contributions?

One of the most helpful strategies in finding these believers is to be as visible as possible in the communities that you serve. It is critically important that the unique and important work that your organization is doing be as widely publicized as possible. In addition to seeking out donors who believe in what you are doing, you want donors to seek you out because of your differentiated approach to solving the important human improvement activity in which they are passionately interested but can't solve on their own. This won't happen if these donors don't know about you. It is absolutely essential that your image in the community be clear, positive, productive, and differentiated if you are to have the passionate donors who will make the greatest difference in your fundraising efforts seek you out. Smaller not-for-profit organizations are in urgent need of these passionate believers.

2. Identify Potential Donors

❏ *1-11: to talk about . . .* After positively differentiating your organization from others in your category of human improvement activity, you can begin to identify the major potential donors. They will be ones who strongly identify with your differentiated philosophy, vision, and mission. Once that is done, you will be able to align the packaging of your differentiation with their needs, interests, and priorities.

The core of your differentiation does not change, but the way in which it is presented does. Here is a partial listing of potential sources of monetary and non-monetary resources for your organization. Make additions to this list that you believe are appropriate.

Interested individuals	Athletic organizations
Clients	Government:
Program participants	• Federal
Patients	• State
Employees	• County
Financial institutions	• Municipal
Businesses	International organizations
Foundations	Venture capitalists
Trade associations	Sources of product philanthropy
Religious institutions	Income from real estate
Service clubs	Endowments
Family associations	Trust funds
Colleges and universities	Investment portfolios
Professional organizations	Institutional fundraisers

3. Learn More about Potential Donors

❏ *1-12: to carry out . . .* You can begin this process by listing all the donors who have contributed in the past as well as those who might possibly contribute in the future.

After identifying potential sources of funding, it is important that you learn as much as you can about each of them. What is their philosophy? What are their beliefs and values? How do they perceive themselves; i.e. what is their self-concept? What is their mission? What are their goals and objectives? Who are the decision-makers? What is their history of providing resources? What organizations have they given to and for what purposes?

As part of this research process, you may find it useful to construct a chart such as the one depicted in Figure 1.2. Rate each of the categories on a scale of 1 to 3 — with 1 representing high potential, 2 representing average potential, and 3 representing below average potential.

NAMES OF POTENTIAL DONORS	POTENTIAL INTEREST IN YOUR ORGANIZATION	SHORT-TERM GIVING POTENTIAL	LONG-TERM GIVING POTENTIAL

Figure 1.2
Ratings of the interest and giving potential of possible donors

Thorough, in-depth research is essential to successful fundraising. Do your homework before venturing forth in the quest for financial and non-financial resources.

Differentiation is the key to successful fundraising and resource development for the smaller not-for-profit organization in the 21st century. As we have seen, it serves as the foundation of our relationship with current and potential donors. In today's highly competitive environment, being unique and distinctive is of the essence. Differentiation provides us with the opportunity to be first in the minds and hearts of donors.

Chapter 2 deals with building and mobilizing a Board that fully understands the importance of organizational differentiation in the fundraising process. It discusses the essential characteristics of a "Fundraising Board", shows you what personal qualities to look for in successful Fundraising Board members, how to recruit these individuals, and how to organize, structure, motivate, and sustain the Board's involvement in fundraising while having fun in the process. The training and development of Fundraising Board members is also emphasized.

Smaller not-for-profit organizations will find that Chapter 2, as is true of the other chapters in this book, builds upon the information provided in the earlier part of the book to provide them with the fundraising expertise that is especially relevant to their own unique situations.

Chapter 2

Mobilizing Your Fundraising Board

The beliefs and actions of the Board of Directors of a not-for-profit organization will determine to a large degree the success of that organization in generating financial and non-financial resources. The Board's philosophy, vision, and sense of mission along with the strategies and tactics it employs are central keys to successful fundraising. At the heart of the Board's fundraising strategies must be a commitment to creating a unique and exciting organization that achieves excellence in its field of human improvement work. The Board has to know how to act as the driving force in differentiating its organization from others in the field. The Board has to have the will and the strategic skills to build a unique, differentiated organization that will attract committed, enthusiastic donors. Chapter 2 will show Board members of smaller not-for-profit organizations, and those who work with them, how to achieve these objectives.

Important Questions

❏ *2-1: to talk about . . .* This chapter addresses the following questions about the nature, role and involvement of a not- for-profit organization's Board in the fundraising process.

➢ What kind of Board do you want?

➢ What do you want the Board to do with regard to fundraising?

➢ Why is the Board of central importance in successful fundraising?

➢ What is a Fundraising Board?

➢ How do you organize and structure the Board's involvement in the fundraising process?

➢ How do you identify an individual who would be a good Fundraising Board member?

➢ How can you sustain the Board's involvement in fundraising?

➢ How do you motivate Board members to become actively involved in fundraising?

➢ In what kind of development activities should you engage your Board?

➢ How can you have fun while fundraising?

➢ How can you build a Board fundraising network?

➢ How can you build a culture of Board leadership and participation in the fundraising process?

Define What Kind of Board You Want

❏ *2-2: to think about . . .* The first question: "What kind of Board do you want with regard to fundraising?" is of the essence. If fundraising is unimportant to your organization, you may choose to have a Board that has no interest or skills in this area. You may decide to focus on Board member characteristics that will advance your organization in non-financial, non-resource development ways. But first, define what kind of Board you want!

1. What is a Fundraising Board?

❏ *2-3: to think about . . .* The central importance of the Board in the fundraising process raises the question as to what the make-up of a Board dedicated to fundraising should look like in action. A Fundraising Board should possess the following characteristics:

- Strong commitment to the philosophy, vision, and mission of the organization.

- Ability to see the outcomes that can be achieved with the proper utilization of additional resources.

- Capability to create and oversee a culture that values the continuing development of financial resources as a central strategy in building organizational excellence.

- Achievement oriented.

- Loves the challenge of growing the resources of the organization.

- Sets an example by contributing financial and non-financial resources to the organization.

- Excited about using its creativity to give more people the opportunity to contribute to the success of the organization.

- Is educated about the financial operation of the organization.

- Utilizes outside resource people to help it achieve its fundraising goals.

- Gives the communities it serves an ongoing report card of the outcomes achieved by the organization's fundraising efforts.

2. Why the Board is of Central Importance in the Fundraising Process

❏ *2-4: to think about . . .* If you are, like most not-for-profit organizations, in serious need of more financial and non-financial resources, you will want to give a great deal of attention to the recruitment, development, and sustenance of a Board that values and actively participates in the fundraising process. The active enthusiastic support of the Board is at the heart of successful fundraising in not-for-profit organizations for the following reasons:

- Fundraising involves a philosophy and outlook that begins with the governing body of the organization.

- The actions of the governing body are the visible evidence of this philosophy and outlook.

- Through its actions, the Board demonstrates the importance of hard work, enthusiasm, and perseverance in expanding the organization's resources in the pursuit of enhanced organizational performance.

- The fact that the Board is comprised of unpaid volunteers who are strongly committed to the fundraising process underscores the importance of this function to all the stakeholders of the organization.

- The Board has the legal responsibility for the fiscal well-being of the organization. Fundraising is an important part of this fiscal well-being.

- As the governing body, the Board has a special relationship with the communities served by the organization.

- Because of this special relationship, the Board is an important catalyst for identifying and securing donors.

- Oversight of the CEO is the responsibility of the Board.

3. How to Organize and Structure the Board's Involvement in the Fundraising Process

❏ *2-5: to carry out . . .* Having thought about "what kind of Board you want with regard to fundraising," and what the make-up of your Board should look like in its vitally important role, the following strategies are recommended when implementing this process:

- Use the fundraising process as a way to develop an understanding on the part of Board members and other stakeholders of the not-for-profit organization and its mission.

- Create a fundraising group led by the Board of members who serve one-year terms. These terms are renewable if an individual is excited about continuing.

- Use this group as an educational training vehicle for the development of Board members.

- Include Board members, administrative personnel, other employees, donors, community members, and other stakeholders as constituents of the fundraising group.

Recruit Members for that Board

1. Characteristics to Look for in Recruiting a Fundraising Board Member

❏ *2-6: to think about . . .* How does one create a Fundraising Board? What characteristics should you look for in the individuals who will form your Fundraising Board? It is recommended that you look for the following characteristics in people being considered:

- Is passionately committed to the philosophy, vision, and mission of your organization.

- Is outcome oriented.

- Likes a challenge and is achievement oriented.

- Has a track record of having helped other organizations develop and expand their resources.

- Is strongly motivated to improve the human condition.

- Is open to new opportunities.

- Has had a personal experience with the benefits that your organization provides.

- Believes that the outcomes achieved are primarily a result of the effort that is expended.

- Has the attitudes, skills, and competencies needed to work effectively in groups.

- Possesses good communication skills.

- Has the conceptual ability to see the big picture and how the parts fit into it.

- Has demonstrated stamina and perseverance in achieving goals.

2. How to Interview a Potential Fundraising Board Member

❏ *2-7: to think about* . . . Having identified a potential Fundraising Board member, the next step in the recruiting process is to arrange for an interview. It is recommended that the Board Chairperson, along with a second individual selected by the Chairperson, participate in this interview process. This will emphasize the importance of the Board selection process and provides for an increased opportunity for dialogue with the potential Board member. A good interview should provide the opportunity for the following things to take place. Review these items prior to the interview in order that they will be covered during your time with the candidate:

• A thorough discussion of the philosophy, vision, and mission of your not-for-profit organization emphasizing that it is a unique and exciting organization that does exceptionally important work.

• An in-depth review of the previous year's written report of the outcomes achieved by the organization.

• A discussion of specific ways in which the potential Board member's needs and wants regarding being a volunteer can be realized by being a Board member of your not-for profit organization.

• A discussion of the impact of the organization's efforts in improving the quality of the lives of several identified clients of the organization (permission should be secured in advance to do this from the clients involved). These stories provide a powerful, personal testament to the important work of the organization.

• An opportunity for the potential Board member to ask questions regarding the operation of the Board and your not-for-profit organization.

- An invitation being extended to the potential Board member to attend a meeting of the Board in order to meet the Board members personally and observe an actual board meeting in operation.

The following should *not* be part of the interview process:

- Giving the potential Board member the "hard sell."
- "Twisting the arm" of a potential Board member to "do you a favor" and become a Board member, when the individual isn't really interested.
- Understating the requirements of the job in order to get the potential Board member to accept.
- Asking a person to become a Board member because of your friendship with that person, when the person isn't interested.

Remember the characteristics to look for in recruiting a Fundraising Board member as you interview a Board candidate. You are looking for Board members who are strongly committed to the philosophy, vision, and mission of your organization. If this is not true of the potential Board member you are interviewing, move on to another candidate.

> One [additional] word of advice is in order regarding the *recruitment* of "high tech" and other volunteers: Don't recruit volunteers with the purpose of extracting money or equipment from their company. Rather, recruit volunteers for their creativity, imagination, competencies, and brain power. A genuine interest in a volunteer's abilities and competencies is a compliment to that person; an interest in the person which is focused only on extracting money and equipment is just the opposite. (Brown & Ruhl, 2003, 197)

Prepare Your Board Members for Their Roles

1. Their Training and Development

Once You Have Them—Boards find themselves with members who are personally overextended, overcommitted, often overworked—and this is before they become Board members. This is suggested by the rule that states: "80% of the work is done by 20% of the people." That condition then finds its way into meetings and committee sessions. These folks find themselves often confused by a different jargon (NFPs are different from for-profits), by at times confusing information thrown at them in unfamiliar terms. . . . Small wonder some new Board members are absent often or just stop coming to meetings. The well-run Board sees to it that new members are given a formal welcome along with some sort of Board-member training, and that the training continues throughout their time on the Board. After all, the NFP organization is little different from other organizations in that new things are happening regularly, and change is constant no matter how seemingly insignificant the issue. (Brown & Ruhl, 2003, 74-5)

Training—Usually refers to efforts aimed at preparing employees for job-related requirements. People need to know about their organization, its mission and their place in it (orientation) as soon as they begin their job. . . . (Brown & Ruhl, 2003, 156)

Assuming that you have done a competent job of recruiting, what next? You probably have people from all walks of life, people who are professionals and those who are otherwise occupied or employed. Given the nature of most not-for-profit Boards, you should start new members with appropriate training that deals with the nature and work of the organization. As suggested above, there can be any number of types of training that could form a useful part of your organizational efforts. Your task is to prepare those who will be conducting fundraising for their efforts.

Once your training has helped members become comfortable with the organization and its basic workings, development of your Board members, as defined below, should become a regular part of your Board's operations—if you want to keep Board membership interesting and a challenge.

> *Development*—for those in professional, technical, and other highly trained positions, development may take the form of expanding on their current careers, *developing* new insights and skills that will take them into higher levels of performance, or even preparing for a change into a new and different career path. . . . (Brown & Ruhl, 2003, 156)

❏ *2-8: to carry out . . .* New Board members arrive with a spirit of "I'm here, make use of my talents." Take advantage of that spirit through the design and execution of your training and development process. Consider how you are structuring the Board's involvement in the fundraising process. Think back over the many characteristics you have looked for during your recruiting process, making an inventory list for each new Board member as you discuss how that person can be of particular service to the organization. You will then be in a position to design that person's training and development process. Doing so will help you shape the organization's Board into the one you want and need to be ready for the formidable fundraising process you are about to undertake.

2. How to Motivate Board Members to Become Actively Involved in the Fundraising Effort

We come now to the question that has been most puzzling to fundraisers in not-for-profit organizations. How does one motivate Board members to become actively involved in the fundraising effort?

When the word *fundraising* is mentioned at not-for-profit Board meetings, the reaction is frequently one of flight and avoidance. The very sound of the word causes anxiety along with a negative reaction. This is why we have been stressing the importance of (1) creating a Fundraising Board comprised of people who possess certain pro-fundraising characteristics, and (2) of implementing strategies for organizing and structuring the fundraising process. Having done these things, the day-to-day motivation of Board members to actively participate in the fundraising process on a continuing basis still remains an important issue. In short, how does one keep Board members "turned on" to fundraising?

❏ *2-9: to carry out . . .* The list of possibilities suggested here to keep Board members "turned on" to fundraising is long, but hardly all-inclusive. Check off those that seem particularly useful in your specific situation. As other ideas come to mind, add them to the list you have developed.

____ Have a unique and important philosophy, vision, and mission that each Board member passionately believes in; recruit and select board members with this goal in mind.

____ Conduct a Board brainstorming session on a yearly basis to identify a broad range of fundraising projects. When processing these ideas, look especially for those that are directly related to the mission of the organization which are repeatable.

___ Have different recipients of the mission attend each board meeting and tell their story about how the mission has benefited them.

___ Have Board members individually meet with beneficiaries of the mission.

___ Get families of Board members involved in specific fundraising projects along with the Board member.

___ Emphasize fun in fundraising projects.

___ Give significant forms of recognition to the Board for its fundraising.

___ Publicize the results of Board fundraising efforts in the community.

___ Target some specific Board fundraising events to benefit employees of the organization. This will reinforce the concept of fundraising as an important ongoing part of the organizational culture.

___ Report on fundraising achievements at each Board meeting.

___ Stress to the Board the challenge and excitement of helping donors to achieve important results that they couldn't achieve on their own.

___ Conduct at least two workshops a year that focus on different aspects of the fundraising process. Include all Board members in these workshops along with other key stakeholders.

___ Create a partnership between the Board chairperson and the CEO that gives top priority to fundraising efforts.

___ Display fundraising results permanently in the NFP organization's facilities to emphasize that the organization has a culture of fundraising.

___ Create a youth fundraising group sponsored by the Board, that includes some Board member children and grandchildren, that is recognized in the community for its good work.

___ Involve Board members in giving awards to various stakeholders of the organization for their fundraising efforts.

___ Emphasize working in Board member teams.

___ Hold Board sponsored receptions and open houses for current and potential donors.

___ Involve Board members in creating educational materials about the importance of the outcomes that can be achieved with appropriate funding.

___ Idea:

___ Idea:

___ Idea:

3. How Can the Board Have *Fun* in the Fundraising Process?

❑ *2-10: to carry out . . .* An important part of *keeping Board members turned on to fundraising* is providing opportunities to have fun in the process. The idea of fundraising actually being fun would seem to be a radical concept to many people. They believe that fundraising is sheer drudgery and, by its very nature, an onerous, depressing process. Fundraising can, in fact, be a lot of fun. Talk about this openly during your meetings and planning sessions. Then, if you are willing to go along with that premise, what remains is for you to come up with ways that will generate "fun" during your organization's fundraising efforts:

So here are some things you can do to generate "fun" throughout the fundraising process:

- Participate with a team of people you enjoy working with on projects.

- Try to figure out why a particular individual or organization would want to donate to your not-for-profit organization. Such detective work can be a lot of fun.

- Conduct a contest to see how many fundraising ideas your team can think of that relate to the mission of your not-for-profit organization.

- Hold parties to recognize achievements in the fundraising process.

- Have each member of your fundraising group write down one amusing fundraising story and share this personal experience with the other members of the group.

- Organize an annual fundraising idea contest to select the fundraising idea that would be the most fun to carry out.

- Involve celebrities you would like to meet and get to know in the fundraising process.

- Have a contest to see who can develop the most amusing training video about the fundraising process.

- Give fun rewards for achievements in the fundraising process.

- Idea:

- Idea:

- Idea:

Sustain Your Fundraising Board

1. How to Sustain the Board's Involvement in the Fundraising Effort

❏ *2-11: to carry out* . . . A serious problem in fundraising is sustaining the Board's enthusiastic involvement in the fundraising effort over an extended period of time. What happens all too often is that Boards get off to a good start in the fundraising process and then fail to keep the momentum going. It is a sad thing to see a great deal of hard work go down the drain as a Board loses interest in fundraising. Not only is the success of current projects undermined, but the sense of failure that develops sets a negative tone for the future.

This does not have to happen. Current successes can be used as the foundation for future successes. The following strategies are recommended in order to sustain the Board's enthusiastic involvement in the fundraising effort:

• Have a different Board member chair the fundraising effort each year. This Board member will have served as a member of the fundraising committee the previous year.

• Permanently recognize the Chair of the Fundraising Committee with a framed color photograph in a highly visible place in the not-for-profit organization's facility.

• Publish a printed report of the Fundraising Committee's efforts each year and distribute this report widely.

• Hold an annual Board-sponsored event each year, showcasing the outcomes achieved through the organization's fundraising efforts.

• Require that the Chairman of the Board must have served at one time as the Chair of the Fundraising Committee.

• Others:

2. How to Build a Board Fundraising Network

❏ *2-12: to talk about . . .* The Board should take the lead in building a network of donors who provide financial and non-financial resources to your not-for-profit organization. As mentioned previously, the Board is in an excellent position to perform this function, given its knowledge of the community and its people. There are a number of ways in which your Board can facilitate the creation and development of a fundraising network. Check off those below that might work in your situation. Then use them for discussing this topic with your Board.

___ Have a brainstorming session or sessions with the Board to build the network.

___ Create a competition to build the network. (Which Board member can identify the most prospects?)

___ Have Board members rank order (prioritize) prospective donors with regard to the potential for giving.

___ Ask Board members to identify the prospective donors they would be willing to personally contact.

___ Ask Board members to identify potential Board members who would enjoy the fundraising process and be good at it.

___ Have a specific Board member or Board member committee in charge of building the Board fundraising network.

___ Hand out pins or other forms of recognition for participation and/or achievement in the Board fundraising network. Identify levels of achievement.

___ Have members of the Board fundraising network prepare fundraising materials (including educational materials) about the organization's mission, etc.

___ Have the Board fundraising network sponsor various events and activities such as art exhibits, investment clubs, investment seminars, etc.

___ Help potential donors generate income (some of which would be contributed to the organization).

___ Involve the Board fundraising network group in developing a fundraising plan.

___ Involve the Board fundraising network group in reporting on the important outcomes being achieved with the monies that are raised.

There are, obviously, more ways in which this effort to sustain involvement can be extended, and you are encouraged to add your own ideas. Suffice it to say, this effort to prepare your Board members for fundraising activities is of extreme importance if your fundraising efforts are to be successful, stimulating and on-going.

Chapter 3

Developing a Plan of Action
that Gets Fundraising Results

Good planning is at the heart of the fundraising process. The development of a plan that identifies the fundraising goals and objectives of your organization for a specific time period is critical. These goals and objectives must be in line with your unique, important, and exciting mission. Your plan serves as your GPS for fundraising. This road map may have to be altered as you proceed along the way, but the framework for action is in place.

Many small not-for-profit organizations neglect the planning function. This is a big problem because these are frequently the organizations with the fewest resources who would benefit the most from a solid planning effort. One often hears individuals in small not-for-profit organizations say, "I don't have time to plan, I'm too busy dealing with day-to-day emergencies." The reality is that many of these emergencies are the result of a lack of planning. Small not-for-profit organizations, more than other organizations, need to establish priorities, identify and utilize resources, and develop systems that enable them to maximize their fundraising and resource development efforts. The planning process makes it possible for small not-for-profits to zero in on the key resources and systems they need to do the job. This enables them to focus their fundraising efforts on acquiring these resources and establishing these systems. This priority setting process serves as the foundation of the planning process.

A key aspect of fundraising planning is building into the process mechanisms for getting feedback concerning how well you are doing. Are you getting the targeted number of donors? Are contributions being made according to your projected timetable? Are new donors being acquired at the anticipated rate? Is the breakdown of industrial and corporate donors as expected? Do the donor statistics agree with the demographics you have projected with regard to occupation, age, gender etc.? Chapter 3 focuses on the role of priority setting, resource identification and acquisition, and systems development in the fundraising planning process. Performing these functions with excellence provides the foundation for superior performance.

Major contributions were made to this chapter by Dr. Howard Brown, the co-author of the book, *Breakthrough Management for Not-for-Profit Organizations: Beyond Survival in the 21st Century* (Brown and Ruhl, Praeger, 2003). Dr. Brown's insights concerning priority setting, resource identification, acquisition, allocation, and systems development should prove to be of great value to the reader of this chapter. The author has attempted to incorporate Dr. Brown's contributions to Chapter 3 in a manner that results in a thought provoking treatment of the planning function for small not-for-profit organizations.

Important Questions

❏ *3-1: to think about . . .*

> ➤ What are your priorities for fundraising based on your mission and the nature of your organization?

> ➤ How do you become aware of the need to change fundraising priorities?

> ➤ How do you identify the resources you need to do the job?

> ➤ What do you need to think about when you design systems to support the fundraising effort?

> ➤ What are the components of an effective fundraising plan?

> ➤ Who should be responsible for developing this plan?

Develop Priorities

A Case in Point:

The Board of Community Resources Inc. (CRI), a small not-for-profit organization, just could not make any progress because all that seemed to happen during Board meetings was that people talked all around the issues at hand but never (1) came to any conclusions, and (2) never took any action on what was discussed. All sorts of questions and the regularly heard "soap box orations" continued to be barriers to their taking any meaningful strides toward what they desperately sought: mechanisms whereby they could effectively raise money.

"But we really do need to do some fundraising. Our monthly income from the services we provide is just managing to cover our operating costs, and if rates aren't increased next year or, heaven forbid, the state decides to level-fund as they have been threatening, we'll be in some real trouble. And to make things worse, after we took that hit last year, our reserve fund is at its lowest in the past several years."

That conversation, and several like it, had been heard around CRI for the past several years. The Board Chair and the CEO often sniped at each other, figuring the problem was the other's, and that each was really responsible for finding more funding whenever the outlook turned bleak. Once again, it was fall and the next agenda item was "fundraising."

Before the Chair could get much beyond announcing that they were going to really get into the issue of fundraising, "something we really need to get serious about," he was inundated with the usual comments: "What are we really doing now?" "What do people in the community think about us as an organization?" "Do they think we don't need any money since our rates are so high?" "What do we offer—in spite of what our mission statement says?" "We have a reasonable amount of money coming in from operations, so why should anyone want to give us money?" "Haven't we started that new idea we talked about, the one that could generate more cash?" "If we go out and ask for money, what should our 'story' be? What kind of emotional tug can we put out to the public?" And the same old discussion was off and running.

While discussing the meeting the following week, the Board Chair and the CEO decided that they would join forces to get to the heart of the problem they were having with these endless, do-nothing conversations that produced nothing but frustration. So they signed up for a number of sessions at the national convention that was to be held the following month, sessions that took up a number of different ideas dealing with fundraising for not-for-profit organizations. Much to their surprise, they found many attending from other organizations suffering in the same doldrums. On the other hand, there were people there from organizations that had vital fundraising operations, raising lots of money, and willing to talk about what they were doing. Many organizations were small, hadn't been in operation for a long time, had staffs that were so overworked that they didn't have time to deal with fundraising, but still had to learn more about it. There were organizations that might have had a person assigned part-time to do some fundraising, perhaps with assistance from an external professional fundraising organization. And then there were the large organizations, often with multiple sites, who had their own full-time people who ran very professional fundraising operations. With resources like these in the sessions the CRI people attended, there was much they were exposed to, and much they took home for future use.

Back home, after some careful planning, the Board Chair and CEO again placed "fundraising" on the agenda for the next meeting. There was grumbling to be heard when "item 4, fundraising" was announced by the Chair. But before the usual weary litany had a chance to get going, a handout was distributed among those attending. It had these five items on it, with spaces left after each item so notes could be scribbled in them:

1. <u>What kind of organization</u> do we have?

2. <u>Who establishes priorities</u> for our organization?

3. What are our <u>priorities for fundraising</u> (development)— based on our mission?

4. What <u>actions</u> do we think we need to take?

5. What <u>changes</u> in priorities do we foresee over time?

A silence fell as Board members pondered the questions and then sat back—waiting. They realized that someone had upped the ante for this meeting's discussion!

The CRI people are representative of so many found on small not-for-profit Boards everywhere. So let's think through the issues behind the five questions posed at that Board meeting in order to focus on what *priorities* have to do with fundraising.

1. Define What Kind of Organization Yours Is

❏ *3-2: to think about . . .*

There are several basic types of organizations for which fundraising might be considered, and the differences are substantial. Consider the three most often found:

1. Funding comes from a number of reliable sources.

2. Only your fundraising skills and success determine whether your day-to-day operations will be able to continue and whether your mission will have a chance of being fulfilled for another period of time.

3. You are "in business" essentially to carry out one specific operation/program, and then to close down operations—once your mission has been completed.

❏ *3-3: to carry out . . .* After thinking a bit more about these three situations, check off the one that best describes your organization.

___ 1. You are fortunate enough to have your funding coming from a number of reliable sources. Fundraising efforts can be aimed at special projects; rainy-day savings for "nice-to-haves." The funds generated often provide the difference between "basic" and "well-rounded" or enhanced programming.

___ 2. Your fundraising skills and success will determine whether your day-to-day operations will be able to continue. When that is the case, several important considerations must be taken into account:

- Funds raised are to be directed into operating funds and capital items that are necessary in order to continue in business.

- Cash flow scrutiny will become mandatory in order to know where you are heading, and how current cash must be used in the present in order to get there. Such activity will also highlight where and when shortages will become problematic.

The use of existing resources must be maximized (which might reduce the perceived need for fundraising *for the moment*). However, you must realize that existing resources, once depleted, are gone for good and will have to be replaced in the future, or done without.

___ 3. You are "in business" essentially to carry out one specific operation/program. In this situation, thorough planning up front will allow funding needs to be identified, resources brought together and carefully utilized. Careful watch must be kept to prevent changes in plans that will lead to confusion and/or financial overspending.

2. Decide Who Establishes Priorities for the Organization

The "who" is often taken for granted. However, when fundraising is the issue, it is worth revisiting this question. So who will be involved in the ongoing process of determining your priorities, your organization's main concerns and things of most importance or urgency?

❏ *3-4: to carry out . . .* With this in mind, evaluate the role each of the following groups will play in your fundraising efforts. Once that has been done, be sure all involved are in agreement, or at least well aware of the "game plan."

• **The Board of Directors (Trustees)**

For any NFP organization, they are the ones with the responsibility for the mission and its accomplishment, along with the priorities for making it happen.

• **The President/CEO (Executive Director, Administrator) and the management team**

They are the ones who conduct the day-to-day operations that follow directly out of the Board's pronouncements.

• **The people who provide your funding**

Private sources will usually give at least some indication of how they would like their funds to be expended. Governmental agency(ies) will usually be specific as to how their money is to be used, often requiring exact accounting (even periodic audits) to provide assurance as to the final utilization.

• **Those for whom and toward whom your mission is directed**

Who knows better what needs to be done, provided and dealt with, than those toward whom your mission is directed? If there are some of these people serving on your Board, they could provide major input. If there is an advisory group, it too could provide a large assist in setting priorities.

3. Determine What Your Priorities Are (for Fundraising/Development)

❏ *3-5: to think about . . .* Priorities established beforehand will allow you to articulate them (their values/benefits) to those involved in doing the fundraising as well as prospective donors.

"This is *what we need* and this is *why we need it*" should be the essence of your message when approaching someone for help and/or donations. If you are not clear about either of these items, you are not ready to start your fundraising efforts. To not have these priorities determined beforehand is like going hunting with a double-barreled shotgun and having no shells in the chambers!

Carefully consider the following items as you develop fundraising priorities for your small not-for-profit organization:

• Determination of your organizational need.

• Laying out the specifics of what that need "looks like.

• Definition of what will be needed (money, physical goods, etc.).

• Definition of how much of each will be necessary.

• Statement as to how and where this money will be used.

• Determination of when the various needs will be required (a time line helps).

• Agree on why a donor(s) should (or might want to) give to your organization.

• Development of your "case" (to illustrate your need).

• Other:

• Other:

❏ *3-6: to talk about . . .* Here are some additional issues to consider in getting your priorities straight.

____ We know what our organization's stance (the Board, top management, major constituency) is vis-à-vis fundraising. One long-time fundraising consultant regularly asks: "Are you willing to repel some prospective donors in order to attract others? To take a strong stance that accurately describes what it is that you are looking for—what you stand for—when such a stance may turn-off some people?"

____ Our priorities:

- Are professional-sounding rather than "slick" or hokey.

- Are "resource raising" rather than dollar raising.

- Clearly explain "what we need and why we need it."

- Show our intent to stay the course over time.

- Demonstrate our intent to take the path less traveled.

- Demonstrate our organization's flexibility.

- Build trust that will help to make things happen (win-win situations as opposed to win-lose ones).

- Show our sincerity.

____ Our priorities are set in the "landscape" or world climate in which we live *today*. How many times do we hear people talking about "the good old days"? Unless there is a point to be made by discussing what used to be done, or "what we did back when we were kids," stay away from such reflections. Most people or organizations to whom you will be turning for funds are operating from the present out into their and your future. You need to make your priorities fit into their outlook.

___ Any collaborative efforts involved have been well thought-out and clearly stated. If so, include them in your priority listings and be sure they are seen as such. Most donors like to see people and/or organizations banding together to get things done. Usually this means that the cost of such efforts will be lower as a result of economies of scale, shared effort, and quantity discounts in purchases.

___ We emphasize why our organization is worthy of funding, (especially when we are a "stand-alone" organization going up against a multiple-organization group). Some funding agencies may have a preference for collaborative efforts (see above), so it will be up to you to demonstrate why you should receive the funds being requested.

___ We know who we are going to approach, why, and when. For what reason? Here again, setting your priorities at the outset makes sense. It seems that many organizations want to "do it all." However, unless there is a full-time staff with limitless energy, choices will have to be made. There are many groupings of donors, many localities in which donors are to be found, and demographics that can be usefully called into play. But unless someone sets some guidelines to direct the efforts of those who will be carrying out the effort, wheel-spinning may well be the result, causing the outcome to be far below expectations.

4. Actions You Will Need to Take

❏ *3-7: to carry out . . .*

The following actions need to be taken as part of your fundraising efforts:

• Select the person(s) who will run the fundraising process and its various activities.

- Make certain that your board Chairman, CEO, and fundraising people are enthusiastically behind the work to be carried out.

- Decide what is to be asked for . . . and why.

- Determine who you are going to go after . . . and why.

- Decide who and what will be your audience(s) for (1) written materials, and (2) in-person presentations.

- Determine how much visibility will be necessary in order for you to be kept in the public eye.

- Use networks and networking.

- Examine periodically (twice/year if possible): "What has changed?" "What new directions?"

- Control regular expenses: minimizing them is money in your pocket, and that much less to be raised otherwise.

- Calculate the cost of raising this money so you will be able to state that x% is actually going toward the fundraising project's stated purpose.

- Thank people (numerous times), answer their questions, mention their names whenever appropriate—personal attention matters!

- Don't spend huge amounts of time on the "obvious" givers (yet not forgetting to treat them as the important people they are). Instead, invest significant time in developing those who have given small amounts but can give more and those who have significant potential but haven't yet reached their potential.

5. Change Priorities Over Time

It is almost cliché to say that change is difficult, change is painful and change makes most people at the very least somewhat anxious while waiting to find out how it will affect them. The small not-for-profit organization must be pro-active in making changes in its fundraising strategies and tactics if it is to be successful in a rapidly changing fundraising environment. To fail to make these changes could have fatal consequences.

❏ *3-8: to think about . . .* That being the case, work on the following in order to keep your priorities fresh and up-to-date.

* Work toward consistency in your fundraising outlook and program—while still being ready and willing to make changes for a good reason(s).

* Appreciate the power of culture. What went into the building of that culture is important to know and understand as one goes forward to present that organization to potential backers. It should go without saying that there are people who have a major psychological investment in the organization, and their roles should be taken into consideration as changes are considered. You cannot, however, allow these people to stall any and all change processes with the oft heard "we've never done it that way around here."

* Follow your strategic plan, if you have one. If you don't, develop one or some sort of tactical/strategic planning device. But do not be tied to it to the point of rigidity. Revisit it often; keep it a dynamic instrument, one that is useful as opposed to an anchor that holds you to one spot in time.

* Make use of demographics and psychographics available to you. Realize that they, too, change over time, and adjust accordingly as they indicate variations taking place in your environment.

* Continuously keep in mind and examine the landscape around you.

* Whether or not you sense change in the air, periodically (twice/year is good) examine what has changed, what

possible new directions you should be considering, and where you should be heading today and tomorrow.

Each time you do this, keep your strategic/tactical plan in mind as you:

- Assess how you are doing while working to fulfill requirements concerning your stated organizational mission and fundraising goals, and

- Then make any changes needed to keep the organization current and on target while fulfilling today's, and then tomorrow's, mission.

The small not-for-profit organization that keeps its eye on what is taking place around it and acts accordingly, will be able to establish priorities that can keep it vibrant and able to fulfill its mission oriented fundraising goals in troubling times, as well as in easier and more enjoyable times.

Identify Needed Resources

❏ *3-9: to think about . . .*

➢ What resources do you need to do the fundraising job with excellence?

➢ Do you need these resources on a continuing basis or only from time to time?

➢ How do you determine when resources are no longer needed and when new resources are required?

Figure 3.1 identifies some of the resources your small not-for-profit organization will need to accomplish its mission with distinction, and some of the ways you can secure these resources. Keep this diagram in mind as you read about the process of identifying needed resources.

KINDS OF RESOURCES							
INTELLECTUAL	SPECIFIC SKILLS AND COMPE-TENCIES	PHYSICAL LABOR	TECHNOLOGY	MATERIALS AND SUPPLIES	FACILITIES	FINANCIAL	OTHERS
WAYS OF SECURING THESE RESROUCES							
RECEIVE GIFTS AND DONATIONS	BARTER	PAY FOR THEM	RECRUIT VOLUNTEERS WHO CAN PROVIDE THEM	DEVELOP SKILLS IN PRESENT EMPLOYEES/ VOLUNTEERS	RE-ALLOCATE CURRENT RESOURCES	SELL CURRENT UNNEEDED RESOURCES TO OBTAIN THEM	OTHERS

Figure 3.1
Kinds of resources and ways of securing them

The Case Continues:

The discussion at the recent CRI Board meeting turned out to be useful in that the members began confronting issues contained in the five questions posed to them. Once they settled to the task, they did so with CRI's mission and vision statements in hand, noting possible changes to each.

If they thought that would end the conversation, they were disappointed, since the Chair and CEO had other things in mind. The agenda for the following meeting included three items: (A) define and examine our internal financial abilities, resources, assets; (B) look at our fundraising capabilities; and (C) evaluate our community, and make a list of other organizations that might be competing for the same resources.

"Do all this at one meeting?" was the leading comment as the members drifted into the meeting room. The Board Chair was quick to mention that, of course, such questions would take more than one meeting. So they began by setting up three task forces led by (1) the Chair of the Finance Committee, (2) the Chair of the Fundraising Committee, and (3) the staff member who dealt with community/public relations. Board members were then distributed into the three groups, and the discussions began. By the end of the meeting, each group had come up with a number of questions to shape their next discussions. Each agreed that their questions suggested a starting point, that they pertained to their organization, and that they needed more time to work through the issues formulated that evening.

The meeting ended with the progress reports. Each task force announced the date and time for its next meeting at which their work would continue. Each group was encouraged to consider the organization's capabilities as they pertained to their assigned areas.

❏ *3-10: to carry out . . .* So let's start with some questions (as the people in our case did). You can do this with three task forces (as the CRI Board did), or in three separate discussions conducted with your Board as a whole.

Issues for your financial task force to consider:

➢ Is our internal, financial organization (people) well organized? Is it fully staffed? Does it know what it is doing?

➢ Do we have appropriate financial systems in place to deal with all our non-fundraising transactions and our fundraising efforts?

➢ Are all our sources of money well documented and known? Is our Board cognizant of these sources and their uses?

➢ Are audits conducted regularly and understood by all involved?

➢ Is our organization regularly involved in research into potential sources of money, tangible resources, and other identified assets?

➢ Do we work hard at collecting needed data, carefully handling and storing the data, and making use of it?

With that discussion concluded, a look into how you are set up to undertake fundraising efforts is in order.

Issues for your fundraising task force to consider:

➢ How many fundraising leaders are in our organization? How many others will step up and put in a lot of effort given the right leadership?

> ➢ How many other community "movers and shakers" does our board have on it?

> ➢ How do we rate our Board as to its interest in, and willingness to do fundraising?

> ➢ How good a group of volunteers do we have who are willing to assist with our efforts?

> ➢ Have we built and named an ongoing, internal fundraising organization/group/association to develop and carry out our efforts?

> ➢ Are we working with a professional, paid fundraiser?

External people and organizations that are, or might become, involved need to be identified and evaluated during the third discussion. Your standing in the community (reputation, professional status, potential contributors, etc.) should be assessed. Begin by considering the following issues:

Issues for the community/public relations task force to consider:

> ➢ Are we known throughout our geographical region? Do people understand our mission?

> ➢ Is our reputation sound; are we known for our professionalism?

> ➢ Do our employees speak well of us as an employer; do they recommend us to their acquaintances as a good place to work?

> ➢ Do the people within the professional organizations and associations with whom we currently interface and work

consider our people to be competent, and our work professional and appropriate?

➢ Are we aware of the organizations with whom we compete? Do we have good relationships with them? Do we work with and/or consult with some of them on appropriate projects and/or share information with them?

➢ How do we relate to federal, state, and local government(s) and their agencies?

➢ How do we relate to trade and/or professional unions?

➢ How do we see ourselves relating to these organizations and people as potential partners or collaborators?

These questions are certainly not the only ones that can or should be asked. Your organization will have its own: ones suited to the situation, timing, and needs that relate to the important areas/topics that must be explored for your particular situation.

Put Systems in Place

Peter Drucker in his book, *Management: Tasks, Responsibilities, Practices,* says the following about organizational design, "To obtain both the greatest possible simplicity and the greatest "fit," organization design has to start out with a clear focus on key activities needed to produce key results. They have to be structured and positioned in the simplest design. Above all, the architect of organization needs to keep in mind the purpose of the structure he is designing." (pages 601-602) Drucker's observations are relevant not only to organizational structure per se but also to the various systems within the organization, including those directly related to fundraising.

In the fundraising process when a number of steps are connected in such a manner that a change in one step creates a change in the whole process we have a fundraising system. The fundraising system will also be influenced by the systems within your organization such as the business planning system, the funds-accounting system, the community relations system, and the benefit dispersal system.

❏ *3-11: to think about . . .* The development of well thought through fundraising systems is critical to the success of your fundraising efforts. Having well thought through systems in place will enhance your fundraising efforts in the following ways:

1. Provide greater consistency.

2. Enable you to reach more potential donors.

3. Save you time.

4. Involve more volunteers.

5. Improve decision-making by requiring fewer decisions.

6. Reduce complexity.

One of the myths about systems is that they have to be cold, impersonal, uncaring, and inhumane. The reality is that well designed systems enable the people who are always a part of these systems to spend more time in the service of others because they have more time to do so.

The Case Concludes . . .

Upon reconvening, the three task forces—financial, fundraising, and community/public relations—discussed their work to date at some length. Their reports about fundraising priorities and available resources led to a further discussion about the systems that needed to be in place in order to move the fundraising process along. At this point the three task forces decided to work as one group to facilitate the sharing of ideas from all of the members. The group knew that if priority setting, resource allocation, and systems development are done well, the fundraising effort has a high probability of success. They also knew that careful attention to these functions by a highly committed, highly motivated group of people provides the strong foundation that supports continuing success in fundraising.

Systems that Support an Effective Fundraising Effort

❏ *3-12: to think about . . .* Let's look now at systems that support a successful fundraising effort.

- **A system of Board member involvement**

    Board involvement can't be left to chance. A system must be in place to guarantee this involvement irrespective of who is on the Board.

- **A donor research system**

    Research about present and potential donors has to be an ongoing process. This is a non-stop, continuing effort.

- **A system that assesses the changing external environment**

    The external environment (landscape) of the small not-for-profit organization is always in flux. Opportunities and threats in this environment need to be recognized and acted on.

- **A community feedback system**

  Special attention needs to be given to processing feedback from the communities served by your organization as part of your assessment of the external environment.

- **A priority setting system**

  Priority setting cannot be left to chance. Decisions must be made in a timely manner following a systematic analysis of available options.

- **A resource allocation system**

  Available and potential resources must be identified and allocated in a manner that maximizes the positive impact of your organization's vision and mission.

- **A marketing system**

  A continuing effort must be made to discover client needs, develop services and products to meet these needs, deliver these services and products to the clients who need them, and receive feedback concerning the outcomes of these efforts.

- **A function coordinating system**

  A system is required to see that your fundraising related systems support each other in order to achieve maximum success. Conflicts existing between systems need to be eliminated.

- **Funds-accounting systems**

  Accurate records need to be kept of all financial transactions relating to the fundraising process. In addition to providing an up-to-date picture of your efforts, these records provide the basis for reporting to your donors.

+ **Control systems**

  With sound control systems in place your small not-for-profit organization will be able to make the adjustments needed to stay on track regarding your stated priorities and budget projections.

+ **Systems of collaboration**

  Processes of collaboration need to be spelled out in detail and agreed upon in advance in order to avoid conflicts and misunderstandings. This is also necessary in order to keep collaborative efforts focused on agreed upon goals.

+ **A grant allocation system**

  Getting the resources that are raised to the intended recipients in an efficient and timely manner is of the essence. To fail to do so undermines the credibility of your fundraising efforts.

This chapter has focused on the role of priority setting, resource identification, acquisition, and allocation, and systems development in the fundraising planning process. Planning involves developing and analyzing alternative solutions to meeting fundraising needs. It is essential that numerous solutions be developed and examined in order to achieve the best possible solution. In order to do this the participants in the planning process need to exercise a high degree of creativity. Small not-for-profit organizations because of their limited number of employees are in a good position to involve a high percentage of these employees in the planning process in ways that encourage their individual and group creativity. To do so is of the essence since the planning function is of critical importance to success in the fundraising process.

Chapter 4

Building Fundraising Alliances and Partnerships

Important Questions

❏ *4-1: to think about . . .*

> ➢ How do you determine when it is advantageous to enter into an alliance or partnership for fundraising purposes?

> ➢ What qualities and characteristics should you look for in a fundraising partner?

> ➢ What are the obstacles that deter people and organizations from entering into alliances and partnerships?

> ➢ What fears deter people from entering into alliances and partnerships?

> ➢ Should partnerships be more than "fundraising partnerships?"

> ➢ How do you create trust in partnerships and alliances?

> ➢ How do you achieve clarity of image for your partnership in the mind of the donor?

> ➢ How do you create an effective decision-making structure within your fundraising alliance or partnership?

A central question in fundraising and resource development is whether to proceed on one's own, or to enter into a partnership (usually involving two parties) or an alliance (thought of as involving more than two). The alliance or partnership could be with another not-for-profit organization, a private sector for-profit organization, a public entity, or with a combination of these organizational forms.

It is becoming increasingly difficult for not-for-profits to attract needed financial and non-financial resources on their own. A major reason for this is the significant increase in the number of not-for-profit organizations needing to generate the resources to support themselves. This increased competition for funding forces a not-for-profit organization to carefully examine alternative ways to attract resources. One of these ways is to build fundraising alliances and partnerships. There is, however, much to consider before entering into such a partnership. The sections that follow will help you think through the issues, and how to deal with them.

Individualism versus Cooperation

❑ *4-2: to think about . . .* When considering the potential of becoming part of an alliance or partnership for fundraising purposes, it would seem useful to first examine one's attitude toward "going it alone" versus cooperating with others. The history of the United States has a long tradition of individualism. Individual achievement and recognition have been and continue to be strongly ingrained in our culture. But one also needs to consider the advantages of working closely with others.

Take a minute to examine your attitude toward *working alone versus working with others* and your need for *individual recognition.* Where does your attitude lie on each continuum?

Working Alone vs. Working with Others		
strongly prefer working alone	equally comfortable working alone or with others	strongly prefer working with others
your assessment:		

Individual Recognition		
extremely important	moderately important	unimportant
your assessment:		

The Environment of the Not-for-Profit Organization

❏ *4-3: to think about . . .* In addition to the increased competition for resources due to the proliferation of not-for-profit organizations, there are other factors (in the internal and external environments of the contemporary not-for-profit organization) that argue for the desirability of participating in alliances and partnerships for fundraising and resource development:

• Accountability for the efficient and effective use of resources by eliminating unnecessary overhead expenses and duplication of effort.

• The increasing need to work together because of greater interdependency in a global society.

• Changing funding priorities that favor cooperative efforts.

- An increasing demand for high-impact results that can only be achieved by multiple organizational involvement.

- An increased demand by both the public and private sectors on not-for-profit organizations to provide services that they do not wish to provide themselves, or cannot provide as well.

- An inadequate organizational capacity to generate resources that will meet an expanding societal need.

- Operating in a world of technology that provides immediate feedback concerning outcomes, which in turn creates an impatience for immediate results.

Potential Advantages and Disadvantages of Alliances and Partnerships

❏ *4-4: to talk about . . .* After surveying forces in the external and internal environments that support or oppose entering into alliances and partnerships, it is important to identify potential advantages and disadvantages of such cooperative efforts. As you read over this list, see if you can add to it.

Advantages

- Increases available monetary and non-monetary resources.

- Forces one to look at and clarify one's values, goals, and objectives.

- Helps to develop relationships that go beyond fundraising and resource development.

- Develops an organization's ability to be trustworthy and to work cooperatively.

- Forces one to re-assess one's position in the external environment (landscape).

- Attracts new donors.

- Increases the pool of fundraising ideas.

- Expands the number of fundraising options.

- Permanently expands the fundraising base.

- Reduces the duplication of requests to donors.

- Attracts donors who value cooperative efforts.

Disadvantages

- Increased level of complexity.

- May compromise organizational uniqueness.

- May threaten the independence of the organization.

- Could create tension and conflict.

- Could undermine clarity of image.

- Decision-making may become more difficult.

- May require a longer time to take action.

- Could result in a compromise in values.

Questions to Consider before Entering into an Alliance or Partnership

❏ *4-5: to talk about . . .* Upon completing your review of the potential advantages and disadvantages of alliances and partnerships for fundraising and resource development purposes, there are a number of specific issues that need to be considered concerning the desirability of your organization participating in such a cooperative effort. Consider the following, and check off the ones you feel most strongly about. You may then wish to add others that relate to your particular circumstances.

***We believe that our alliance or partnership has
a good chance to . . .***

___ Raise more money for our organization.

___ Result in an increase in non-monetary resources.

___ Move our organization ahead in achieving its goals
and objectives.

___ Be a positive experience for all of those who participate.

___ Increase the number and range of donors.

___ Allow our organization to achieve a higher level of perfor-
mance and contribution than we could achieve on our own.

___ Strengthen our image and reputation in our category of
human improvement work.

___ Energize our employees to increase their contributions to
the work of the organization.

Overcome Psychological Barriers to Creating Alliances and Partnerships for Fundraising and Resource Development

❏ *4-6: to carry out . . .* In the process of analyzing the
potential advantages and disadvantages of entering into an alliance or partnership for the purpose of fundraising and resource
development, you should be aware of several psychological
variables that may be present. These variables may affect your
objectivity and serve as barriers to effective decision-making—
they are lack of trust, and fear.

Psychological Barrier 1: *Lack of Trust*

First look at lack of trust. How trusting are you in your relationships with other people and organizations? Mark on the continuum where you perceive yourself with regard to trust.

Self-evaluation — How trusting are you?				
don't trust anyone	rarely trust	trust people about half of the time	trust people most of the time	trust everyone
your assessment:				

An awareness of your tendency to trust or not to trust is important as you think about the alliance and partnership process. Don't allow your inherent tendencies to cloud your objectivity in analyzing the potential value of fundraising alliances and partnerships.

Should you decide to enter into a fundraising alliance or partnership, there are a number of ways in which you can increase your own capacity and the capacity of others to trust. This will result in an alliance or partnership in which trust is a central ingredient of your success. Here are some considerations for you to think about:

How to build trust

- Respect the organizational uniqueness of your partners as well as your own uniqueness.

- Act in a trustworthy manner; consistently do what you say you are going to do.

- Strive for win-win outcomes—moving to a higher level than one could on one's own.

- Develop a thorough knowledge of the culture of your fundraising partner(s).

- Allow each partner the freedom to act creatively, to achieve mutually established goals in creative ways.

- Develop a familiarity, a sense of kinship.

- Have a strong mutual vision.

- Identify mutual interests that go beyond the raising of money.

- Identify and build on common areas of organizational philosophy.

- Be open, honest, and up-front in your dealings.

- Develop friendly personal relationships—the personal dimension of trust.

- Build a track record of cooperative behavior one step at a time—a culture of trust.

- Develop a common organizational language.

- Develop a decision-making structure that engenders trust.

Psychological Barrier 2: *Fear*

Fear is another psychological variable that may affect your objectivity in thinking about potential alliances and partnerships. Fear may take a variety of forms. It can create obstacles and cause inertia in the building of alliances and partnerships. Becoming aware of your fears and their immobilizing effect on the decision-making process are first steps in moving toward more objective analysis and action. Consider these fears (and add others you can think of to this list).

Fear of:

___ Not being Number 1.

___ Being blocked from performing the mission which you believe you are uniquely qualified to do.

___ Not being recognized for your achievements.

___ Disappearing—of losing your identity.

___ Being taken advantage of.

___ Becoming mired in organizational red tape.

Qualities and Characteristics to Look for in a Fundraising Partner

❏ *4-7: to carry out . . .* If your research and analysis argues persuasively for the desirability of entering into an alliance or partnership for fundraising and resource development purposes, what qualities and characteristics should you look for in such a partner or partners?

It is recommended that you use the following compatibility index. You will find it worthwhile to rank these qualities and characteristics on a scale of 1 to 5, with 5 being the most favorable rating from your point of view. Have each partner do so, and then compare and discuss the outcomes.

Qualities and characteristics we are looking for in a fundraising partner

___ Has mutual interests that go beyond the raising of money.

___ Possesses complimentary differences.

___ Has a compatible mission.

___ Has a compatible culture.

____ Has a compatible image.

____ Has a compatible style.

____ Has a compatible personality.

____ Has compatible fundraising goals.

____ Is trustworthy.

____ Has a donor base that, combined with ours, will excite additional donors.

____ Demonstrates a commitment to excellence.

____ Demonstrates, through action, a value system of cooperation.

____ Demonstrates a high level of competence.

____ Has a willingness to share the spotlight.

____ Demonstrates honesty and openness of communication.

____ Possesses sound organizational health.

Fundraising Partners in Different Sectors of the Economy

❏ *4-8: to think about . . .* Your not-for-profit organization may decide to collaborate with another not-for-profit organization, a for-profit organization, a public sector (governmental) organization, or with a combination of these organizational forms. When collaborating with any organization, it is important to understand that organization's characteristics.

Characteristics of organizations in different sectors of the economy

Not-for-profit sector

- Private organization led by volunteers.
- Involved with improving some aspect of the human condition.
- Excess income invested in the work of the organization.
- Frequently perceived as a part of government.
- In many cases has an unclear image.
- Sometimes perceived as duplicative.
- Often has fewer resources to work with than private or public sector organizations.

For-profit sector

- Profit driven.
- Frequently exhibits an impatience for results.
- Expected to contribute to the broader society (social responsibility).
- Has shareholders to whom it is accountable.
- Perceived as being focused and effective.
- Often perceived as being self-serving.
- Sometimes perceived as being destructive to the environment.

Public (governmental) sector

- Accountable to the public.
- Frequently accountable to elected officials.
- Funded by taxpayers.
- Frequently perceived as being inefficient.
- Often perceived as being bureaucratic.
- Sometimes perceived as employing political hacks.

As mentioned previously, when collaborating with another organization, a knowledge of the characteristics of the sector with which the organization is affiliated is important. This knowledge will provide a useful background for understanding in greater detail the specific reasons why the collaboration is sought and how you can best assist your partner in meeting the desired goals and objectives.

For example, if you are working with a **public sector (governmental) organization**, it is important to communicate to the public being served that your public sector partner is performing efficiently and effectively with important outcomes being achieved, if such is in fact the case. This recognition will be appreciated by the elected officials who need to be re-elected if they are to continue in office and will serve to counteract the common perception that public organizations are inherently bureaucratic, inefficient, non-responsive, and wasteful.

When collaborating with a **for-profit organization**, it is important to stress the social concern of that organization in working with your not-for-profit organization to improve the human condition. This will be greatly appreciated by the for-profit organization as it helps to counteract the image that private sector organizations are self-serving, uncaring, and oblivious to the needs of the broader society.

If the collaboration is with another **not-for-profit organization**, emphasize the fact that this is a case where two not-for-profit organizations are working together in order to maximize the impact of the efforts being undertaken to improve the human condition. This collaboration will demonstrate that this is an important non-governmental effort with a clear mission in which not-for-profit organizations are working together in a non-duplicative manner, while maximizing scarce resources.

Select a Specific Project on Which to Collaborate

❏ *4-9: to carry out . . .* Once your organization has secured a partner or partners to collaborate with in the fundraising and resource development process, the next step is the identification of specific projects on which you wish to collaborate. Some important questions to ask in the project identification process are:

➢ Is the project related to the philosophy, vision, and mission of the participating organizations?

➢ Is the project differentiated?

➢ Are all the participating organizations passionately committed to the project?

➢ Is the time and effort required to successfully complete the project warranted by the results that can be achieved?

➢ Is the project too complex?

➢ Can a joint decision-making structure be implemented that is simple and effective?

➢ What is the potential repeatability of this project in the future?

Projects should be distinctive. They shouldn't be the same old boring projects that everyone else is doing. The fundraising event should ideally be related to the purposes for which the organization exists. This is best done if the theme of the event is directly related to the organization's mission. An example of this would be a local historical society whose annual fundraising dinner focuses on the food, music, and events of a particular year in the history of the community. The work of the organization deals with history and the specific fundraising event deals with history. If the fundraising event doesn't thematically deal with the mission of the not-for-profit organization, the mission can be introduced through sub-events. An example of this would be a golf tournament at which an annual award is given that relates to your organization's mission. If your organization is a long-term care facility, an annual award could be given to the individual who has done the most in your service area to contribute to the quality of life of older citizens. Some aspect of a fundraising event should always be linked to the mission of the not-for-profit organization. Developing this link is a great way to increase your creativity.

Develop Working Arrangements

❏ *4-10: to carry out . . .* Prior to actually embarking on a specific project, decisions need to be made regarding the following partnership issues:

➢ What is the decision-making structure?

➢ Who makes the decisions?

➢ Who is in charge?

➢ Who speaks for the partnership?

➢ What are the commitments of each of the partners?

➢ How are outcomes measured?

➢ Who does the measuring?

➢ How is information shared?

➢ How is recognition handled?

➢ What is the duration of the partnership?

➢ What is the process for ending the partnership?

Create a Compelling Image of the Partnership in the Mind of the Donor

Donors and potential donors may or may not be aware of the individual organizations that are working together, but they will most certainly not be aware of the goals and objectives of the new fundraising partnership itself. Thus it becomes very important to create a compelling image of the partnership in the minds of donors.

❏ *4-11: to carry out . . .* To achieve this compelling image, it is recommended that you:

___ 1. Communicate about the exciting project on which the partnership is about to embark.

___ 2. Stress the advantages of the joint action:

 ♦ Better utilization of resources.

 ♦ Expanded impact.

 ♦ Elimination of duplication of effort.

 ♦ Increased donor base.

 ♦ Sharing of complementary strengths.

 ♦ Increased visibility.

 ♦ Increased idea pool.

 ♦ Underscored importance of the human improvement work being undertaken.

The Partnership/Alliance

❏ *4-12: to carry out . . .*

1. Maintaining the partnership/alliance

As the fundraising partnership moves into full operation it is important that the participating organizations institute the following practices:

- Keep the partnership vision, mission, and goals clearly in mind.

- Share information widely about the work in progress.

- Report frequently about the outcomes being achieved.

- Celebrate successes.

- Recognize individual and group contributions.

- Emphasize, support, and recognize the culture of cooperation that has been created.

- Maintain and strengthen personal relationships.

- Orient and train partnership participants on a continuing basis being certain to include new members.

2. Ending the partnership/alliance project

When a fundraising project has been successfully completed, the following actions are recommended as part of the process of concluding the project:

- Identify and celebrate the accomplishments of the project.

- Make a commitment to work together again on appropriate projects in the future.

- Recognize the project participants.

- Publicize the accomplishments of the project.
- Reward superior project performance.
- Develop and put in place a process for identifying future partnership projects.
- Identify ways in which a future partnership project can be even better than the one just concluded.
- Make a commitment to stay in touch on a regular basis.

It is important that a fundraising project end with a good feeling—toward each other on the part of the participants, and toward the effort that has been made to achieve the fundraising goals and objectives. This good feeling lays the groundwork for future successful fundraising projects.

Chapter 5

Using High-Impact Communication to Raise the Money You Need

Important Questions

❏ *5-1: to think about . . .*

> ➢ What should you be communicating?

> ➢ With whom should you be communicating?

> ➢ How do you communicate—*with impact*?

> ➢ What are the best communication vehicles for you to use?

> ➢ How do you develop a coordinated, consistent message?

> ➢ How do you achieve interactive communication?

Communicate

❏ *5-2: to carry out . . .*

Communicate About Your Differentiation

In order to achieve outstanding results in the fundraising and resource development process it is essential that a not-for-profit organization communicate in a compelling, motivating manner. The organization's unique, distinctive, and important mission must be communicated with a passionate enthusiasm to the individuals and groups who constitute a potentially receptive audience.

This is an area in which many not-for-profit organizations fall short. When asked why a not-for-profit organization needs money the answer is often inadequate. Even when an organization has an important exciting mission there is often a failure to communicate the impact of its work in improving the human condition. There is a failure to connect with the intellectual and emotional needs of the donor. Buying acid free boxes for a history museum or wheel chairs for a nursing home does not generally excite the passionate enthusiasm of potential donors. Stories about how contributions positively impact the lives of people for the better do evoke such passionate enthusiasm.

❏ *5-3: to carry out . . .*

Communicate with the Right People

As discussed in Chapter 1, the identification of receptive audiences of donors must be systematically pursued. In-depth research about potential donors must be a top organizational priority. A chart such as the one depicted in Figure 1.2 can be extremely useful in analyzing the potential of prospective donors. It is important to remember that a not-for-profit organization shouldn't attempt to appeal to everyone. Don't waste time, effort, and energy communicating with those who are not interested in your unique identity and mission.

Build two-way communication networks with those who identify with the important work you are doing. Your differentiated image must be aligned in the communication process with the needs and interests of potential donors. It is essential that you show those you are communicating with how to achieve goals and objectives which are important to them that they can't achieve on their own. Your differentiated image must be communicated in a clear and consistent manner. This exciting, motivating, differentiated image communicated to current and potential donors serves as the foundation of your fundraising and resource development efforts.

Know, and Be Part of Your Community

One important way of identifying and communicating with individuals and groups who are interested in the work your organization is doing is to become an integral part of the communities that you serve. It is important to do this on both an organizational and a personal level. Community involvement enables employees to represent your organization in the community; to be the face of the organization in an action sense while at the same time locating those people who are truly interested in your mission and work. Personal communication in the form of concrete actions taken is the most powerful kind of communication. The involvement of your organization and its people in specific community improvement projects related to your mission sends the message that your organization does what it says it does. The Salvation Army is an excellent example of an organization that identifies community needs and then takes action to meet these needs even if all the necessary funding isn't in place. Funding is sometimes requested after action has been successfully taken. The completed project is used as a success story to attract the needed resources.

High community visibility often results in individuals and organizations stepping forward to help because they have come to understand the contributions being made by your organization to the well-being of their friends and neighbors. An organization that serves a number of communities needs to develop strategies for interacting with all of these communities at the local level. Just as "all politics is local" so too is "all fundraising local." National and international agendas of not-for-profit organizations gain passionate and enthusiastic support at the local level. It is at this level that the message really sinks in and is converted into the giving on the part of donors that makes the achievement of a not-for-profit organization's goals and objectives possible.

High-Impact Communication

Communicating through actions is central to effective communication. What you do is more powerful than what you say if there is an inherent conflict between the two. However what you say and how you say it is also of critical importance. The following eight action strategies are recommended to achieve high-impact communication:

❏ *5-4: to carry out . . .*

1. Use the Creative Pyramid

It is highly recommended that you use the creative pyramid as developed by Arens in formulating a powerful message to current and potential donors. The steps in the creative pyramid are: 1. Attention, 2. Interest, 3. Credibility, 4. Desire, and 5. Action. The first step is to capture the attention of potential donors. The second step is to arouse interest on their part in contributing to the important work that your organization is doing. The third step is to establish the credibility of your organization as an important differentiated not-for-profit organization that is achieving outstanding results in improving the human condition in your area of service. The fourth step is to create a desire in the minds of donors to participate in achieving the vision, mission, goals, and objectives of your organization and to be able to picture in one's mind the improvements in the human condition that will be achieved. The fifth step is to get potential donors to take action and make contributions to the work of the organization; i.e. to become donors. The creative pyramid should be kept in mind whenever a message is being developed in the communication process with donors.

❏ *5-5: to think about . . .*

2. Select the Best Communication Vehicles

One of the most difficult decisions a not-for-profit organization has to make in the fundraising process is what communication vehicles to use in delivering its message. The central questions are (1) what are you trying to achieve and (2) how effective will a particular communication vehicle be in achieving these goals? Use the following questions as guidelines in measuring the effectiveness of a specific communication vehicle.

➢ Does it enable you to communicate our differentiated mission?

➢ Will it reach the intended audiences of potential donors?

➢ How quickly will it get results?

➢ Is it cost effective?

➢ Can you afford to use it with some frequency over a period of time?

➢ Can it be used with other communication vehicles to maximize impact?

> ➤ Does it have both intellectual and emotional impact?

> ➤ Does it have the potential to provide us with feedback about donor reaction to our vision and mission?

> ➤ Is the vehicle consistent with the image you are trying to create?

❏ *5-6: to carry out . . .*

3. Emphasize Giving as an Investment

The concept of giving as an investment is a powerful motivating incentive for many donors. Positioning giving as an investment in the mind of the donor is very different from positioning it as a charitable contribution. The idea of investing in something of importance is attractive to many people. Part of this is the concept that the investment will grow thereby expanding its positive impact on improving some aspect of the human condition in the future. Here are some ways in which the concept of giving as an investment can be implemented in the fundraising and resource development process:

- As a way to save money.
- In a cause that is important to you.
- In your sense of self-fulfillment.
- In improving the community in which you live.
- In your health and the health of your loved ones.
- In your children.
- To preserve your name or the names of others who are important to you.

You are encouraged to think about the concept of giving as an investment and to add to the preceding list of implementation strategies.

❑ *5-7: to talk about . . .*

4. Focus On Your Strengths

High-impact communication in successful fundraising is centered on the strengths of your organization. The strengths that need to be communicated about are the ones that form the foundation for your organization's unique, differentiated identity and mission. If, for example, the major differentiating factor about your organization is its truly superb customer service, then consistent ongoing communication about the people who drive this superior performance will be of the essence. If innovation is the major differentiating factor, then your organization's track record of providing innovative products and services should be consistently emphasized. Augmenting and communicating about the strengths that form the basis for your organizational uniqueness requires constant attention. Repetition is of central importance. It is important to keep emphasizing the things your organization does better than anyone else. Focus on these strengths and the outcomes they achieve in improving the human condition.

❑ *5-8: to think about . . .*

5. Utilize Competence-Based Simplicity and Clarity

At the heart of high-impact, high-results fundraising communication are the concepts of simplicity and clarity. The message must be one of simplicity, not complexity; clarity, not confusion. In order to do this, it is necessary to have an in-depth understanding of the mission and ongoing operations of your not-for-profit organization. Lack of understanding results in complexity and confusion. Without understanding, clarity of communication is not possible. The important point to be made here is that the employees and other stakeholders of a not-for-profit organization need to do their homework if they are to be effective communicators. They have to know what they are talking about. High-impact fundraising communication is not "seat of the pants" communication. It is based on *understanding* which promotes *competence* which fosters *clarity of communication* which generates *donor giving* (in the form of financial and non-financial resources) for the institution.

Understanding → Competence
→ Clarity of Communication → Donor Giving

A special word is in order about simplicity of communication. There is an inherent tendency in the communication process to move toward complexity. In an over-communicated society, such complexity is frequently screened out. Simplicity and clarity are required to get the attention of prospective donors, and are essential if an organization is to break through the "noise" of competing requests for resources.

❏ *5-9: to carry out . . .*

6. Be Consistent

In the process of communicating your differentiated image to donors and other stakeholders, the importance of the concept of consistency needs to be stressed. We are talking here about (1) consistency of the message from all the members of your organization, (2) consistency between what is said about your mission and the actions that are taken, and (3) consistency in communicating your organization's core differentiation over significant periods of time.

It is important that everyone in your not-for-profit organization know what your organization is about; what its purpose is, how it operates, how it is unique, and what its impact is on the lives of people. In addition, the organization and its people need to do what they say they are going to do to improve the human condition. If there is a conflict between words and actions it is the actions that affect the perceptions of donors and potential donors. The third important aspect of consistency is to communicate what the essence of your differentiation is and to stay with it. Many not-for-profit organizations change their message with such frequency that their identity is seriously undermined.

❏ *5-10: to carry out . . .*

7. Emphasize Two-Way Communication

The goal in the communication process is to create a strong, positive interactive relationship between the *not-for-profit organization* and its *current and prospective donors.* Further, it is important that this exchange takes into account the intellectual as well as emotional needs of all involved.

Two-Way Communication

Not-for-profit organization ←→ Donors

(strong positive interactivity which is both intellectual and emotional)

Try these suggestions for implementing this strong, positive two-way communication process with donors and prospective donors.

- Use the "personal touch" whenever possible.
- Involve donors in setting goal priorities where appropriate.
- Utilize mechanisms for donor feedback.
- Involve donors in work on projects.

- Provide opportunities for donors to communicate with the recipients of services.

- Involve organization members and donors in mutual recognition activities.

- Practice pro-active listening.

- Do what you say you will do.

❏ *5-11: to carry out . . .*

8. Tell Stories

Stories concerning the positive impact of not-for-profit organizations on the lives of people can have a very powerful effect on donors and potential donors. These stories should appeal to both the heart and the mind. The stories told can be about positive changes in the lives of individuals, groups, communities or other entities. The goal is to get donors and potential donors to identify with the people in the stories who have been helped by your organization. The ideal is for these donors to project themselves into the situation being described in the story. The stronger this identification with the people in the story and the benefits they have experienced as a result of the work of your not-for-profit organization, the better.

Powerful Points for High-Impact Communication

❏ *5-12: to carry out . . .*

Provided below is a checklist of powerful points for high-impact communication. Use this list to review the information presented in this chapter and to implement the specific actions you will take to achieve high-impact communication with present and potential donors.

Checklist of Powerful Points for High-Impact Communication

___ Begin by having a clear, brief, motivating, high-impact mission statement.

___ Use employees as communicators of your vision, mission, and goals.

___ Practice integrated marketing communication where everyone in your organization is on the same page.

___ Differentiate your organization on major, important issues.

___ Be passionate about the work you are doing.

___ Utilize the power of "enlightened self-interest" in creating donor activity and contribution.

___ Creatively recognize donor contributions, promptly and often.

___ Make use of benefit recipients in communicating your message.

___ Develop real connections with your donors: Do research, identify the words that will connect with them, then focus on effective delivery and interaction.

Specific Techniques for Effective Communication with Your Donors

• Communicate how you are different and better in your category of human improvement activity; your uniqueness within a conceptual framework.

• Use personal stories that show your impact on the human condition.

• Use action as a way to communicate—actions speak louder than words.

- Use nonverbal communication in its many forms.

- Use upward, downward, and lateral communication.

- Strive for simplicity and clarity; emphasize consistency; be sincere.

- Use both rational and emotional approaches.

- Be sensitive to the different cultures of various donor constituencies.

- Listen and watch carefully to be certain that your message is being accurately perceived.

- Identify things that get in the way of receiving your message and overcome them.

- Deliver your message frequently.

Any good reference book will note that "communication" is a complex concept involving effective speaking, active listening, and good feedback. This chapter has discussed strategies and techniques that will enable the small not-for-profit organization to utilize high-impact communication to secure badly needed contributions of time, assets, and money.

Chapter 6

Sustaining a Culture
of Successful Fundraising

Important Questions

❑ *6-1: to think about . . .*

➢ How does one sustain the fundraising process in a changing environment with changing participants?

➢ What do we mean by the term, *culture*?

➢ Why is culture an important concept in fundraising?

➢ What shared assumptions form the groundwork for sustaining a fundraising culture?

➢ What do we mean by the term, *stakeholder*?

➢ How does one motivate these stakeholders to participate actively in the fundraising process?

➢ What do we mean by "enlightened self-interest"?

➢ Why is the Board Chair – CEO relationship of central importance in fundraising?

➢ How do you develop a commitment to fundraising throughout the organization?

➢ How do you encourage innovation in fundraising?

➢ Why is recognition such a powerful motivator in the fundraising process?

➢ Why is it of critical importance to get the resources raised to the intended recipients?

The Power of Culture in Fundraising

❏ *6-2: to talk about . . .*

If a not-for-profit organization is to be successful in fundraising over an extended period of time, it must create an organizational way of life that supports such fundraising. Another name for this organizational way of life is culture. The culture of the organization is comprised of shared values, beliefs, norms, and assumptions that are embedded in the fabric of the organization. The culture is the very essence of the organization. Its members have "bought into" a set of shared assumptions about "how things are done around here." These assumptions are clearly understood even though they may not appear in writing. The significance of culture in sustaining successful fundraising is illustrated below.

Why culture is important in sustaining fundraising

Culture is the way of life of an organization. In order to sustain successful fundraising, certain shared values, beliefs, and assumptions need to be in place. Many of these shared assumptions about what is important and how things are done are unwritten and taken for granted. They drive the behavior in the organization.

The following determinants of sustained, successful not-for-profit fundraising are directly related to the culture of your not-for-profit organization:

- Organizational uniqueness.
- Commitment to mission.
- Role of leadership.
- Decision-making behavior.
- Commitment to performance excellence.
- Level of innovation.
- Extent of employee participation.
- Extent of stakeholder participation.
- Sensitivity to the needs of employees and other stakeholders.
- Extent of and forms of organizational recognition.
- Importance given to meeting the needs of the customer.
- How success is defined.
- Value given to cooperative behavior.
- Support of creativity.

What shared assumptions about organizational performance and contribution support a culture that values and successfully raises financial and non-financial resources? What shared assumptions support ongoing fundraising rather than sporadic one-shot efforts? What shared assumptions overcome the fundraising inertia experienced by so many not-for-profit organizations? What shared assumptions provide a foundation for creative, imaginative, impassioned fundraising?

The following shared assumptions are fundamental in forming the groundwork for sustaining a fundraising culture. They include a deep belief in:

- The inherent worth and growth potential of the individual and the need to create an environment in which human potential can be realized.

- The importance of the work your organization is doing in improving the human condition which allows human potential to be realized for the benefit of society at large.

- Achieving excellence in organizational performance through expanded resources in order to meet the needs of as many potential clients as possible.

- Giving as many people as possible the opportunity to achieve their goals by contributing to the work of your organization.

Managing the Fundraising Culture—the Importance of Leadership

❏ *6-3: to think about . . .*

Leadership is of critical importance in managing the fundraising culture. Of special significance is the leadership of the Board Chair and the Chief Executive Officer (CEO). It is essential that the Board Chair and the CEO work as a unified, committed team in creating, leading, and sustaining a fundraising culture in the not-for-profit organization. This team is of critical importance for the following reasons:

- This is the team that leads and unites the policy formulation and operational functions of the organization. Successful fundraising is a matter of both policy formulation and operational implementation.

- This is the team that has to be in agreement if sustained, successful action is to be achieved.

- The public pronouncements and actions of the Board Chair and the CEO are watched closely by and influence the response of the community to the organization. This response includes financial and non-financial contributions.

- The Board Chair and CEO are instrumental in initiating, implementing, and embedding values in the culture of the organization that sustain successful fundraising.

- This is the team that produces a level of certainty in an environment of uncertainty. A can-do approach to fundraising supports this level of certainty.

- The level of cooperation present in the Board Chair – CEO relationship sets the tone for the level of cooperation present throughout the organization. A strong cooperative effort is essential in successful fundraising.

- The level of trust present in the Board Chair – CEO relationship serves as an example with regard to the level of trust throughout the organization. Trust in the proper utilization of the financial and non-financial resources that are raised is essential to successful fundraising.

- The goal setting of the Board Chair and CEO is of central importance in creating an environment in which the achievement of excellence demands continuous successful fundraising.

Sustain a Culture of Successful Fundraising

❏ *6-4: to carry out . . .*

1. Continue Differentiation

Chapter 1 emphasized that being a unique, differentiated organization with a unique, important, and exciting mission is the
foundation of successful fundraising. In the process of sustaining a fundraising culture it is essential that the uniqueness and
importance of the not-for-profit organization's mission be a top
priority. Many not-for-profit organizations lose their way in a
sea of shifting priorities. They lose their identity and they lose
their ability to raise badly needed financial and non-financial
resources. Don't let this happen to your organization. Keep the
following ideas from Chapter 1 in mind as you work to sustain
your fundraising efforts.

In order to avoid being the same old boring business-as-usual
type of organization that no one wants to support financially:

- Continue to create an organization that is unique, important, and exciting so that it motivates people to provide you
  with money and other resources.

- Be certain that your organization is really conspicuously
  different in an important positive way from your fundraising
  competitors. This will attract and keep excited and committed donors.

- Be certain that your organization's philosophy, vision,
  mission, strategy, and tactics are aligned with each other.

- Use one powerful differentiator that your organization is
  known for to enable it to be first in the minds of the donors
  in your category of human improvement activity. Support
  this principal differentiator with supplemental differentia-

tors that reinforce it, allowing a greater number of potential donors to relate to the work of your organization.

- Look for potential donors who believe in you and feel passionately about the distinctive and important work that you do. Be willing to repel those who don't.

- Align the packaging of your differentiation with the specific needs, interests, and priorities of potential donors without changing the core of your differentiation.

- Use differentiation as the foundation of your relationship with current and potential donors.

2. Commitment to Excellence

❏ *6-5: to think about . . .*

Another cultural determinant of sustained successful fundraising is the not-for-profit organization's commitment to excellent organizational performance in achieving its mission. Excellent performance provides the satisfaction that renews and recharges the fundraising initiative. Excellent performance stimulates additional excellent performance. Being a winner in achieving one's fundraising goals and objectives invites even broader participation in the effort. People like to be associated with a winner. A commitment to organizational excellence is important in sustaining the fundraising effort for the following reasons.

Why a commitment to organizational excellence is important in sustaining the fundraising effort

- Achieving excellence requires developing monetary and non-monetary resources.

- A commitment to excellent organizational performance forces the members of the organization to use their creativity in developing these needed supporting resources. Using one's creativity is a personally rewarding experience that encourages a continuation of effort.

- Excellent performance by its very nature provides a personal satisfaction that renews employee commitment to securing the resources required to do the job.

- Excellent performance develops community support which in turn sustains excellent fundraising performance.

- Donors like to be associated with winners.

- Excellence requires the willingness to try new things which in turn energizes the fundraising process, thereby keeping it fresh and interesting.

3. Innovation

❏ *6-6: to carry out . . .*

The ability to innovate is of critical importance in sustaining the fundraising process. The central ingredient in creating a culture of innovation is an openness to new ideas wherever they may be found. Many not-for-profit leaders, managers, and organizational members are carefully trained in their socialization process to be experts in discovering what is wrong with something. They are educated to be "experts in criticism." Creativity in developing new approaches to fundraising as well as new fundraising products is dependent upon being "experts in withholding criticism" in the initial stages of the innovation process. Early criticism is responsible for the elimination of many potentially productive fundraising ideas. It is recommended that you work to sustain innovation in the fundraising process in the following ways:

- Encourage an organizational mind-set that is open to new ideas.

- Encourage an organizational mind-set of calculated risk taking.

- Emphasize the fact that your organization is on the cutting edge of implementing new and creative fundraising ideas.

- Embed the value in your organization that innovation is exciting and rewarding.

- Emphasize the thrill of being a leader in fundraising innovation.

- Scan the external environment (landscape) in which your organization operates on a continuing basis for new fundraising ideas.

- Use brainstorming techniques on a continuing basis to generate large numbers of fundraising ideas.

- Encourage creativity, not criticism, in your approach to new fundraising ideas.

- Don't be afraid to implement a new fundraising idea after you have done a solid job of research.

- Provide monetary and non-monetary rewards for successful new fundraising ideas.

- Celebrate the success of new fundraising ideas.

- Create a culture that encourages continuous suggestions from employees concerning new ideas in fundraising.

- Develop skills and competencies in adapting new fundraising ideas being implemented by other organizations to the particular needs of your organization.

- Be aware that the environment in which your organization operates is changing all the time and that your approaches to fundraising must also change.

- Be especially careful when you are most successful not to keep doing fundraising in the same old way. Success can cause you to become complacent.

4. Participation

❑ *6-7: to think about . . .*

Participation can be a great motivator because it actively engages the participant in the process at hand. Your involvement as a participant in the fundraising process is at a more intense level than involvement you may have as a spectator. Getting people to actively participate in the fundraising process is a top priority if one's goal is to achieve sustained successful fundraising. The act of participation sustains fundraising performance in the following ways:

• Increases commitment to mission.

• Provides insight into the organization.

• Provides insight concerning the external environment.

• Introduces realism.

• Challenges one to utilize one's potential.

• Challenges one to be successful.

• Builds comradeship.

• Encourages increased preparation.

• Replaces inertia.

• Translates thought into action.

• Provides the opportunity for direct feedback.

• Provides the opportunity to applaud oneself.

• Provides the opportunity for recognition from others.

• Is a prelude to personal and professional growth.

• Provides a sense of satisfaction when others follow your lead.

Role of Stakeholders

❏ *6-8: to carry out . . .*

If the act of participation nurtures and sustains fundraising performance, the question then arises as to how a not-for-profit organization can motivate its stakeholders to participate in the process. A stakeholder is an individual, group, or organization that has an interest in the success of your not-for-profit organization. The identification of current and potential stakeholders is the first step in the process of getting them actively involved. The next step is to figure out how the participation of each of these stakeholders in the work of your organization is in their "enlightened self-interest." In what ways will their participation on your behalf help them to achieve their goals and objectives?

The stakeholders of your not-for-profit organization will most likely include all or some of the following: administrative personnel; the rest of your employees; recipients of your services; suppliers; the communities you serve; municipal, local, state, federal government; partnership and alliance participants; taxpayers; other social service agencies; and professional and accrediting groups and societies. It is in the "enlightened self-interest" of these stakeholders to participate and to continue to participate in the fundraising process if the greater their involvement the greater are the benefits they receive. This process is called the *Fundraising Wheel of Enlightened Stakeholder Self-Interest*. It is recommended that you take the following actions to motivate your organization's stakeholders to participate in the fundraising process.

Motivating Your Organization's Stakeholders

How do you motivate your organization's stakeholders to participate in the fundraising process? Utilize the power of enlightened self-interest.

- Emphasize the financial benefits that they will receive from helping your organization raise money.

- Emphasize how such participation will enhance their community image.

- Link the benefits your clients will receive as a result of the monies raised to some aspect of their organizational mission.

- Demonstrate the broader value to their organization that comes from your organizations working together in areas other than fundraising.

- Give each stakeholder recognition for the positive outcomes achieved through the financial and non-financial resources that are raised.

- Emphasize the opportunities for leadership development that occur as a result of your organizations working together.

- Emphasize the fun that the employees of your organizations can have as a result of working together in the fundraising process.

- Emphasize the excellence that can be achieved in serving your clients as a result of the monies that are raised.

- Emphasize the excitement and sense of accomplishment that the employees of your organizations can experience as a result of working together on an important fundraising project.

5. Recognition

❏ *6-9: to think about . . .*

Recognition is another powerful motivator in sustaining the fundraising effort. Recognition supports our sense of self-worth. A sense of self-worth is essential in providing us with the confidence to reach our fundraising goals. Recognition should be given for both individual and group fundraising achievements. Such recognition renews the "fundraising spirit" and demonstrates that fundraising is valued by your not-for-profit organization. Recognition is important as a motivator in fundraising for the following reasons:

Group recognition

- Gives the members of the group a sense of pride.
- Builds teamwork.
- Increases team morale.
- Provides continuing momentum.
- Provides a sense of completion.
- Develops a success mentality.
- Maximizes individual performance through commitment to larger goals.
- Provides a mutual support system.
- Encourages the idea that the whole (group performance) can be greater than the sum of individual performances.

Individual recognition

- Promotes self-confidence.
- Gives one the confidence to work with others in achieving goals.
- Increases a sense of self worth.
- Encourages enhanced performance.
- Encourages one to continue to perform at a high level.
- Provides energy and enthusiasm for the tasks ahead.
- Encourages a can-do attitude.
- Supports the idea that one can contribute to the group without losing one's identity.
- Encourages personal creativity.
- Serves as a model of excellence for others to follow.

6. Get the Resources that are Raised to the Intended Recipients

❏ *6-10: to think about . . .*

One of the best-managed and most successful not-for-profit organizations is the Salvation Army. It should be no surprise that the Salvation Army is also one of the most effective not-for-profit organizations when it comes to fundraising. At the heart of its fundraising success is the fact that the Salvation Army is a highly differentiated organization with the well deserved reputation of providing its services to the people who need them the most with relatively little money being spent on administrative overhead. The Salvation Army delivers on its promises and in doing so wins the support of its donors. It is extremely important that a not-for-profit organization deliver as large a share of the resources that are raised as possible to the intended recipients for the following reasons:

Why the intended recipients should receive as large a share of the resources that are raised as possible

- Demonstrates that the organization's mission is being accomplished.

- Emphasizes the needs of the clients as opposed to spending money on administrative overhead.

- Reinforces the trust of funding sources in the organization.

- Demonstrates the integrity of the institution.

- Provides the not-for-profit organization with a competitive advantage in soliciting future financial and non-financial resources.

- Demonstrates that the organization is accountable for its actions.

- Energizes the organization's employees to achieve an even higher level of fundraising performance because they can see the significant impact for the better on the lives of the people being served.

- Demonstrates the administrative skills of the organization.

- Demonstrates through action that the not-for-profit organization does what it says it is going to do.

- Meets its public trust responsibilities.

7. Use Successes to Keep the Momentum Going

❏ *6-11: to think about* . . .

The celebration of fundraising successes provides the pathway for more fundraising successes. One success lays the groundwork for another success. Successes should be used to develop a "success mentality"; a can-do attitude that is based in the reality of previous performance. The following ways to use successes to keep fundraising momentum going seem an appropriate way to conclude a chapter on sustaining a culture of successful fund-raising. If one pays proper attention to the cultural determinants of a fundraising culture, successes will occur that can then be utilized in creating additional successes.

How to Use These Successes

❏ *6-12: to carry out . . .*

• Establish specific short-term goals (4-6 weeks) within the framework of longer-term goals.

• Celebrate the successful completion of these goals within the organization.

• Build on these successes—use them as stepping stones.

• Celebrate the successful completion of longer-term goals with events held in the community.

• Recognize both group and individual fundraising achievements.

• Communicate the achievement of substantive goals to appropriate community constituent groups.

• Develop ways of permanently recognizing fundraising achievements.

• Talk about successes in informational materials published by your organization.

• Talk about successes in all media events.

• Keep a visible easily accessible written record of fundraising successes in public places within the organization.

• Demonstrate how specific fundraising successes move the mission of the organization forward.

• Link fundraising successes to the outcomes they help to achieve in the form of improvement in the lives of specific individuals who are served.

- Develop a short, dynamic media presentation focusing on your organization's successes in getting the resources raised to the people who need them.

- Recognize fundraising successes in the compensation system.

In the process of overcoming THE SIX MAJOR BARRIERS TO SUCCESSFUL FUNDRAISING: 1. Being like everyone else, 2. Having a non-participating Board, 3. Reacting only to emergencies, 4. Communicating the wrong message, 5. Participating in one-shot efforts, and 6. Going it alone, your small not-for-profit organization will develop a culture that will support your fundraising efforts. Sustaining the fundraising effort is what it's all about in both good and bad times. There is often a tendency to lose focus in good times. This is a bad thing as fundraising discipline and consistency are undermined leading to serious problems in tough economic times. As has been stressed in this book, building a culture of fundraising is all important! It is the hope of the author that this book will serve as your action guide to building a culture that sustains your fundraising efforts over time.